Go Set a Watchman
Teacher's Guide with
Lessons, Activities and Novel Study

Common Core State Standards Aligned

© 2015 Lucky Jenny Publishing. All rights reserved.
Plymouth, California
ISBN-13: 978-0692513873 (Lucky Willy Publishing)
ISBN-10: 0692513876

Permission to use in single classroom only.

Publisher's Note: This book was made by humans -- if you find errors or typos – please let us know and they will be immediately researched and, if appropriate, fixed.

Table of Contents

A Quick and Dirty Guide to *Go Set a Watchman*	5
Themes	7
Symbols	8
Characters	9
A Quick and Dirty Guide to Literary Elements	10
R.A.F.T. Assignment – Historical Background Assignment	11
Pre-Reading R.A.F.T Student Pages	14
Go Set a Watchman Novel Unit	17
With Summaries and Analysis for Each Section	
Comprehension Quizzes for Each Section	
Historical Non-Fiction Text Assignments	
Other Assignments and Graphic Organizers	
Go Set a Watchman Final Exam	48
Common Core State Standards Literature Assignments	51
Socratic Discussion/Seminar with Rubric	62
Go Set a Watchman Interactive Notebook	65
Templates and Assignments for Universal Access	
Answers and Information	102

A Quick and Dirty Guide to
Go Set a Watchman

Themes

A theme is the underlying meaning of a literary work. A theme may be stated or implied.

Themes	*Go Set a Watchman* Themes
The Co-existence of Good and Evil	In *Go Set a Watchman* nothing exists at the extremes – including good and evil. Their co-existence in the gray area of life and what it means to be human becomes evident as Jean Louise returns home to Maycomb, Alabama to a changing world. To Jean Louise, Atticus is or was the definition of good; however, she quickly learns that her just and good father is a member of a group that harbors racist ideals and the lines between good and evil blur forever in her head and within hear heart. Even Jean Louise is not immune to the co-existence of good and evil within herself as she is implied when she states: *"But Uncle Jack, I don't especially want to run out and marry a Negro or something."* Thus, Jean Louise talks about the importance of equal rights and of being color blind, but marrying out of her race is out of her zone of morality. Racism in the cultural context of the south is this theme to the nth degree. Like in *To Kill a Mockingbird*, the ability to adapt to the co-existence of good and evil and its simultaneous presence is imperative to the understanding Jean Louise comes to of her father as well as the community which is rooted in the core of her being and is key to the ultimate growth she experiences as a daughter and as a person.
Everyone is created equal – or not:	Jean Louise was raised believing that all people were created equally. Over the course of *GSW*, she discovers that the majority in her small town of Maycomb, Alabama does not share these beliefs and that equality is not as black and white as she once believed.
Change:	Change is a difficult, sometimes slow, process. The South is no exception. When the Civil War ended and Reconstruction began – the Black Codes transcended into the Jim Crow Laws – and change did not begin until many, many decades later. Change, in fact, is still an arduously slow process, as Mississippi did not even ratify the Thirteenth Amendment until 2013.
Morality vs. The Appearance of Morality:	Can morals or one's conscience change over time? Jean Louise believes her father to be morally unbreakable and righteous; however she learns that external actions don't necessarily reflect someone's internal principles and that the guise of morality may be deeply seeded within her own family. This theme manifests itself in the relationships Jean Louise has with Atticus and Henry Clinton – as well as in her growing discomfort with Maycomb.
Rules and Order:	If you want to learn about some of the most important and imposing *unwritten* rules in the United States, try attending a social tea in Alabama. The notion of rules and order underlie each action and reaction within GSW.
Race and Racial Inequality:	Race is woven through every page of the GSW. It is complicated, messy and multi-faceted. It is also masked by the perception of what is legal and ethical and marred by arguments of what is best for the whole vs. the individual. Lee touches on a tension within democracy, as the south and the Finch family, as well as all of Maycomb, struggle with individual freedoms and the life they have known vs. equality and the good of the whole.
Gender Inequity:	On the surface Jean Louise is an independent women. She lives in New York, presumably alone. She has a job. She supports herself and she is willful and fiery; however, she succumbs to her aunt's teas and the hierarchy of the men in her life.

Symbols

A symbol is literary device containing multiple layers of meaning, usually concealed at first, and representative of several other aspects, concepts or traits than those that are visible in what is literal, thus, symbolism is using an object or action that means something more than its literal meaning.

Symbols	Symbolism in *Go Set a Watchman*
Arthritis:	Atticus' hands are crippled with arthritis. His deteriorated state is symbolic of the seemingly moral and ethical way he has deteriorated, but has he or are his true feelings merely more apparent. In *To Kill a Mockingbird*, Atticus was the symbol of equality, but signs existed that perhaps imply Atticus harbored, at least in part, the same views of social hierarchy as his sister Alexandra and the rest of Maycomb. He highlights, more than once, that he was charged with defending Tom Robinson, he brings his sister, who he knows lives in a world where social hierarchy is paramount, in to help raise his children. In *GSW*, Atticus emerges as a wonderfully flawed character struggling, like everyone else, with the balance of his needs and ideas vs. those of the people around him. His ailment is symbolic of the flaws discovered by Jean Louise as her father deteriorates from icon to human – over night.
Watchman:	Everyone is his or her own watchman or conscience. In the end, Jean Louise realizes she is her own person and her own watchman. She develops her own identity separate from her father. *"'Go Set a Watchman' means, 'Somebody needs to be the moral compass of this town,'" Flynt said. "Isaiah was a prophet. God had set him as a watchman over Israel. It's really God speaking to the Hebrews, saying what you need to do is set a watchman, to set you straight, to keep you on the right path. What more elegant title could there be?"*
The Car Roof:	The main conflict for Jean Louise is that change is difficult and dealing with change is even more difficult. The car roof is symbolic of Atticus and as Jean Louise metaphorically hits up against her father before she learns that she must work with who he – she too hits the car roof. Jean Louise learns she must work within herself to bend - -because neither the car roof or her father is likely to. In the end, Jean Louise bends to miss hitting her head on the car roof and bends her ideas to consider that her father is the man he always was – complete with the imperfections that accompany being human.
Blindness:	Jean Louise's color blindness, Atticus' blind eye, Jean Louise blind to the imperfections that mark her father as human and Jean Louise blind to who she is inside. In *TKAM*, we see Atticus idealized through the innocent eyes of a 6 through 9-year-old. In *Go Set a Watchmen*, we see Atticus come alive as a person of flesh, blood and faults – he is human now. But we also see Jean Louise profess color blindness – while at the same time saying she would never intermarry.
Slap in the Face	At the end of the novel, when Jean Louise is hysterically leaving, Uncle Jack literally and symbolically slaps her in the face. It is at this point she begins to realize that she is her own person, her father is human, they are not one, she can have her own identity and actually accept who her father is as well – flawed as it may be.

	Main Characters
Jean Louise Finch	Jean Louise Finch, aka Scout, is the protagonist. She is strong and independent – much to her aunt's chagrin wears monochrome pants out in public and flirts with her boyfriend. She has much the same personality as she did when she was nine. She has a definite moral compass and is described as color blind; however, like in *To Kill a Mockingbird,* she is childlike and the product of the southern belle south – as much as she tries to quash it – it underscores who she is. Jean Louise struggles inwardly with her place as a woman in society. She is a good person – who is flawed by a quick temper. Jean Louise discovers a bit about herself as the novel progresses and perhaps grows a bit as well.
Atticus Finch	Atticus is Jean Louise's widowed father. He has a strong sense of morality and justice and seems committed to racial equality – or so one is led to believe in *To Kill a Mockingbird*. Even though he seemingly strives for racial equality, he lives in the world he exists, where inconsistencies around racial interaction abound, that while unjust, he accepts. As the novel progress it becomes less evident that Atticus is indeed as anti-racist as one would believe or if he is a product of the southern world from which he was bred. It is difficult to ascertain if Atticus is truly a States' Rights proponent or a racist southern gentleman. He loves his family though – and he is calm and even-tempered. In the end, he comes across more human than the Atticus of *To Kill a Mockingbird.*
Aunt Alexandra	Aunt Alexandra is Atticus' sister and obsessed with maintaining her place in Maycomb society. She has lived with Atticus since Jem died and now cares for him in his ailing physical state. She is a southern belle and openly racist. She lives what she knows. Her goal is to get Jean Louise to stay home. She can be snippy, racist and it seems she is critical of everything Jean Louise does. While Atticus describes Alexandra as *impossible* – she breaks down at one point and then actually tells Jean Louise she *is* a lady. Alexandra lives in the past, but perhaps this one moment illustrates that she sees the inevitable future and needs Jean Louise around to survive in it.
Henry Clinton	Henry is a boy from the wrong side of the tracks. Aunt Alexandra calls him *trash*. He father deserted him and his mother died when he was young. Atticus Finch took care of him and made sure he had what he needed. He fought in the war, went to college and is now a lawyer beside Atticus. Aunt Alexandra thinks he is a carpetbagger – coveting all that is Atticus'. Jean Louise treats him poorly and her actions show that maybe even she thinks she is too good for him. She teases, flirts and tortures him but admits she could never marry him – not won't marry, but could never marry.
Calpurnia	The Finch family cook when Jean Louise was growing up. She helped raise the children with a stern hand. She moved out when Jem died. Jean Louise goes to see Calpurnia, after her great-grandson accidently hits a man with a car. Calpurnia is distant and cold – illustrating the divide between black and white society in the south in the 1950s. The scene is dark and tense – symbolic of the racial tensions of the time. Jean Louise goes to see Calpurnia, but then forgets all about her. She knows she was raised by a black woman and a white man, but Jean Louise was raised in a society that sees both woman and African Americans as subservient and a thread of this runs through her as well.

A Quick and Dirty Guide to Literary Elements

The literary devices and nuances of *Go Set a Watchman* should be highlighted throughout the course of teaching this unit – as examples become present. Introduce the elements, as they relate to the novel, all at once at the beginning of the unit, after the non-fiction piece, as it is helpful and provides a basis for student understanding.

The Basics

Voice: The novel is written in third person limited, *"She touched yesterday cautiously, then withdrew. I don't dare think about it now, until it goes far enough away."*

Genre: Coming of age. Jean Louise goes homes, discovers grow-up realities such as her southern family may have southern ideals after all, but in the end realizes that she is her own person with her own identity. She becomes her own watchman.

Tone: innocent, naïve, ironic, nostalgic and even critical

Plot Analysis:

- **Exposition:** Jean Louise returns home to Maycomb, Alabama in the 1950s. Racial tensions mount and her father, boyfriend and even uncle are different than the people she thought she knew growing up.
- **Conflict:** Jean Louise discovers that the people she loves, including her just and iconic father, are part of the citizens' council – an anti-racial group, white elitist group and that her father, who always fought for equal justice, really does not believe in applying the concept across the board.
- **Climax:** Jean Louise faces her father, denouncing him and his actions as a hypocrite and racist.
- **Falling Action:** Jean Louise, with the help of her Aunt Alexandra and Uncle Jack, grows to understand that she can't run from what she's learned and that her father is still her father and in the end – she welcomes him to the human race and realizes that she is her own person, with her own thoughts and identity

Social Studies Tie-In: As your students work through *Go Set a Watchman,* discuss the plot in terms of states' rights vs. equality.

Harper Lee throws in several comments about the issue for Atticus being one of states' rights rather than social justice. They are few, but enough to leave the reader wondering what is really at issue for Atticus. Does he truly believe separate is equal or does he believe that it is the individual states' rights to make those determinations.

When Jean Louise remembers her father stating *"She heard her father's voice, a tiny voice talking in the warm comfortable past. 'Gentlemen, if there's one slogan in this world I believe, it is this: equal rights for all, special privileges for none."* (page 108 of first edition) – could it all be untrue really?

Or are Atticus and Uncle Jack more against a large centralized government: *"'Cynical, hell. I'm a healthy old man with a constitutional mistrust of paternalism and government in large doses. Your father's the same –"*

Go Set a Watchman alludes to the conflict between the allocation of power between the state and federal governments. The federal government, established by the Constitution, recognized the importance and the sovereignty of both state and federal governments and granted mutually exclusive power to both – only it also granted concurrent power. At the Constitutional Convention in 1787, delegates knew that state governments had become centers of power. The Constitutional framers purposely avoided a precise definition of the locus of sovereignty – leaving people to infer which had more power. Only, defenders of states' rights were concerned that a powerful centralized government would usurp the rights of the state governments. Accordingly, the Tenth Amendment was added to the Bill of Rights. The Tenth Amendment became the battle cry for states' rights proponents as it states: *"…powers not delegated to the United States by the Constitution, nor prohibited by it to the States, are reserved to the States respectively, or to the people."*

From the early 1800s, states' rights played a major role in the political process and the ideals and structure of the south especially. A South Carolina statesman, named John Calhoun, stated: if acts of the Federal Government ran contrary to those of state or local interests, states had the right to nullify those acts. Calhoun's followers linked states' rights to slavery – therefore protecting slavery meant protecting the interests of the southern states.

When the Civil War ended with the defeat of the South, Congress enacted the Fourteenth and Fifteenth Amendments, partly to prevent states from denying basic rights to citizens of the United States; however, the Supreme Court restricted the power of these amendments during the 19th Century, indirectly of course, using the states' rights argument to justify their actions. This trend continued until the 1930s, with the court using the Tenth Amendment to limit Federal power. In the 1930s, Franklin D. Roosevelt's New Deal policies dramatically increased both the power and size of the Federal government. States' rights were revived in the 1940s over race. In 1948, presidential candidate, Harry S. Truman pushed on a more aggressive civil rights policy. Southern democrats left the party and ran their own candidate, J. Strom Thurmond on a states' rights platform that called for continued racial segregation and against proposals for Federal action regarding civil rights.

Desegregation efforts, up to and including the 1950s, including the Supreme Court's decision in Brown v. Board of Education, which ruled racial segregation in schools was unconstitutional, met with southern resistance – to say the least. Segregationists argued for state sovereignty and developed programs of resistance that included opposing racial integration of education, housing, access to jobs and public facilities.

Challenge your students to read *Go Set a Watchman* through the lens of both states' rights and civil rights – as these tensions of democracy not only play an important role in understanding the context of the novel, but worked to shape the United States of America as it stands today.

PowerPoint: Email publisher@luckyjenny.com for access to the PowerPoint presentation for the following assignment.

Directions for Differentiation of Non-Fiction Pre-Reading Assignment: Discuss the historical context of Harper Lee's *Go Set a Watchman*, go through the PowerPoint timeline, have students read the nonfiction text and complete a R.A.F.T. to demonstrate their understanding of the passage.

What is R.A.F.T.?

Raft is a strategy for providing different options for students to demonstrate their learning. R.A.F.T. is the 1982 brainchild of Dorothy Vandevander and is a great way for students of varying levels to transform content knowledge in engaging and fun ways – as R.A.F.T. allows students to choose the means by which they communicate their knowledge of information learned. R.A.F.T. assignments allow students to discover their own voices and formations for presenting content information.

The benefits of a R.A.F.T. assignment are numerous. Students are asked to display knowledge from a real world perspective and, because they are considering perspective as they go through the writing process, they think more critically and work at a much higher level than when they merely apply the essay writing process.

		R.A.F.T.
R	Role	Students decide their role. They identify their role as the writer or conveyer of information for the task
A	Audience	To whom does the writer speak? What is the audience?
F	Format	What form will a student's response take? How will they demonstrate they've learned the content knowledge at hand?
T	Topic	What is the topic? Ask students to think of the best way to communicate critical information of their topic?

Possible R.A.F.T. assignments for *Go Set a Watchman* pre-reading assignment:

Role	Audience	Format	Topic
Newspaper Reporter	Readers in the 1950s	Obituary	The Death of Segregation
Attorney	US Supreme Court	Appeal Speech	Any of the Cases Listed
Talk Show Host	Television	Talk Show	States' Rights vs. Civil Rights
Advertiser	Magazine Audience	Print Ad	Road Towards Desegregation
Fiction Writer for Children	School children today	Storybook	The History of Segregation
Yearbook Editor	High School Students	Yearbook Entries	Brown v. Board of Education

Raft Rubric				
	4 Mastery	3 Well Done	2. Needs Word	1 Not Yet
Role: How authentic were you in portraying your role? Were you convincing?				
Audience: How well did you address audience's needs? Did you convey the content knowledge in a way that was understandable and engaging to your audience?				
Format: How successful where you in demonstrating your understanding of the content knowledge in the chosen format?				
Topic: How well did your writing demonstrate mastery of the content?				
Conventions: Was your writing, grammar and spelling up to the task.				
Other:				

Name: _____ Date: _____

Go Set a Watchman Pre-Reading Raft

Directions: Read the following passage, choose a R.A.F.T. assignment and demonstrate your knowledge of the **Timeline Towards Desegregation**.

Timeline Towards Desegregation

Figure 1: Sam Scott. Public Domain Image

1857: Dred Scott v. John F.A. Sanford: In Dred Scott, the Supreme Court held that neither free nor enslaved African Americans could be citizens of the United States; therefore, they could not sue in federal court. It also held that the Federal government had no power to regulate slavery in the Federal territories

1865: Bureau of Refugees, Freedmen and Abandoned Lands: Also known as Freedmen's Bureau, this was an act of Congress to help freedmen become self-sufficient. The first black schools were set up under the direction of the Bureau. Howard University was established under Freedmen's Bureau. Note: Thurgood Marshall graduated from Howard.

1865: Black Codes: The Black Codes were laws passed by southern states during the presidency of Andrew Johnson. Immediately after the Civil War ended, Southern states enacted "black codes" that *allowed* African Americans certain rights, like owning property or the ability to marry, but these codes denied them more than they ever granted – such as the rights to testify against whites, to serve on juries or in state militias, to vote, or even start a job without the approval of a previous employer. These codes were all repealed in 1866 when Reconstruction began.

1866: Civil Rights Act of 1866: The Civil Rights Act of 1866 gave African Americans the right to sue, enter into contracts and own property.

1868: The Ratification of the Fourteenth Amendment: The Fourteenth Amendment overruled Dred Scott and guaranteed that all people born or naturalized in the United States are citizens of the U.S., and of the state in which they reside, and that no state could abridge the privileges thereof – including life, liberty or property without due process of law or nor could anyone be denied equal protection under the law.

1873: Slaughterhouse Cases: This series of cases defined federal power and undermined the Fourteenth Amendment by emphasizing that most of the rights of citizens were actually under state control.

1875: Civil Rights Act of 1875: Congress passed the *Civil Rights Act of 1875* banning discrimination in hotels, theaters and places of public accommodation. This was the last Federal civil rights act passed until 1957.

Figure 2: Sign at bus station, Rome, GA from pbs.

1883: Civil Rights Cases: In 1883 the Civil Rights Cases of 1875 were overturned. The Supreme Court declared that the Fourteenth Amendment did not prohibit discrimination by private individuals or businesses – opening the door for further discrimination in public education.

1887: Jim Crow Laws: Jim Crow Laws were state and local laws, imposed in the south, that enforced racial segregation. Nine southern states went so far as to use the law to require segregation.

1896 Plessy v. Ferguson: In Plessy v. Ferguson, Plessy challenged a Louisiana law requiring separate train cars for black and white people. This case is significant because the Supreme Court held that separate but equal facilities did not violate the Equal Protection Clause of the Fourteenth

Amendment. Separate but equal held until Brown v. Board of Education. Plessy had one dissenter, John Marshall, who argued that mandated segregation of the races stamped black people with a moniker of inferiority. This argument would become the crux of the Brown v. Board of Education decision.

1899: Cummings v. Board of Education, Richmond County, Georgia: In Cummings, the Supreme Court upheld a local school board's decision to close a public black school due to budgetary issues, even though it kept two white schools open. The court's decision argued no evidence that the decision was based on racial discrimination but that the distribution of public funds for education was at the discretion of local school authorities. Later cases would impose on local and state rights where Cummings did not.

Figure 3: Public domain image.

1908: Berea College v. Commonwealth of Kentucky: In Berea the Supreme Court upheld a law prohibiting interracial instruction in all schools and colleges within Kentucky.

1909: The NAACP or the National Association for the Advancement of Colored People was founded. The objective of the NAAC was to eliminate lynching and fight

1935: The NAACP Begins to Challenge Segregation: Beginning in graduate and secondary schools, the NAACP – with Thurgood Marshall and Charles Hamilton Houston, began the fight that would overturn segregation in Brown v. the Board of Education. Their fight was two-pronged: separate facilities were too costly for states and separate and segregated black schools were not on the same level, or equal to, white schools.

1938: State of Missouri ex rel. Gaines v. Canada: This was a precedent setting case whereby the Supreme Court decided in favor of Lloyd Gaines, a Black student who was refused admission to the University of Missouri Law School. The court held that the school had to provide an education "substantially equal" to that granted persons of the white race.

1948: Sipuel v. Board of Regents of University of Oklahoma: In Sipuel the Supreme Court unanimously held that Lois Ada Sipuel could not be denied admission to the state law school based on race alone.

1949: Briggs el al v. Elliott et al: Briggs became one of the cases consolidated into Brown v. Board of Education. Briggs was a test case by the NAACP in their efforts to end segregation. Briggs was a class action lawsuit.

1950: Sweatt v. Painter: The Supreme Court held it unconstitutional for the University of Texas Law School to not admit a black student. The Court held that the Texas failed to provide a separate but equal education – foreshadowing the Brown v. Board of Education opinion that "separate but equal is inherently unequal."

1950: McLaurin v. Oklahoma State Regents: In McLaurin the Supreme Court held that Oklahoma's requirement that a black student sit in separate sections in classrooms, libraries and the cafeteria interfered with his ability to interact, study and engage in discussion with other students as well as interfered with his ability to learn his profession.

1950: Bolling v. Sharpe: Bolling became one of the cases consolidated into Brown; however, the Supreme Court would file a separate decision on Bolling because the Fourteenth Amendment was not applicable in Washington D.C. where the case originated. The case involved African-American students not being allowed to enroll in the white John Philip Sousa Junior High School.

1951: Brown vs. Board of Education was filed on February 28 in the Federal district court in Kansas.

1951: May Davis et al v. County School Board of Prince Edward County, Virginia et al: May Davis was a challenge to Virginia's segregated schools and another of the cases eventually consolidated into Brown v. Board of Education.

1951: Briggs et al v. Elliott et al: Briggs went to trail in South Carolina and the District Court denied the plaintiff's request for desegregation, but ordered the equalization of black schools.

1951: Brown v. Board of Education: The District Court unanimously held Brown v. Board of Education stating that there was "no willful, intentional or substantial discrimination" in Topeka's schools, that the facilities were comparable and that the lower court's decision in Sweatt v. Painter and McLaurin applied to graduate schools only.

1952: March Davis v. County School Board of Prince Edward County, VA: The District Court found in favor of the school board under the theory of "separate but equal." In this case, the District Court unanimously rejected the request to order desegregation of Prince Edward County, VA schools, but ordered the "equalization" of Black schools instead.

1952: Gebhart Cases: A Delaware court ruled that the plaintiffs were entitled to admission to white public schools. The court held that the students were being denied equal protection of law. The board of education from Delaware appealed the decision.

1952: The Supreme Court bundled Brown v. Board with the four other cases on school desegregation. This grouping highlighted the issue as being national – rather than one just relevant to the south.

1954: Brown v. Board of Education: The long road to desegregation began in earnest when the Court overturned Plessy v. Ferguson – declaring racial segregation in public schools unconstitutional as it violated the Equal Protection clause of the Fourteenth Amendment.

1955: Brown was a long and arduous fight – ending in Brown II – which was supposed to work out the terms and details of desegregation, but the term "all deliberate speed" was vague and many states threw up legal and social obstacles to thwart integration. These obstacles sparked the flames and acted as a catalyst for the student protests that launched the civil rights movement.

http://www.archives.gov/education/lessons/brown-v-board/timeline.html

Role	Audience	Format	Topic
Newspaper Reporter	Readers in the 1950s	Obituary	The Death of Segregation
Attorney	US Supreme Court	Appeal Speech	Any of the Cases Listed
Talk Show Host	Television	Talk Show	States' Rights vs. Civil Rights
Advertiser	Magazine Audience	Print Ad	Road Towards Desegregation
Fiction Writer for Children	School children in the 2010s	Storybook	The History of Segregation
Yearbook Editor	High School Students	Yearbook Entries	Brown v. Board of Education

Go Set a Watchman
Novel Unit

Part I: Teacher Pages
Part I: Summary and Analysis

Go Set a Watchman opens with Jean Louise "Scout" Finch returning home for an annual visit by train. The opening scene explains how trains have changed since her childhood, foreshadowing the changing world around her, including and centering in her own Maycomb, Alabama. Jean Louis has lived in New York for five-years. Since the time of *To Kill a Mockingbird*, her brother Jem has died, she graduated from high school, attended an all girls' college and moved to New York.

She is expecting her father to greet her at the train station. Instead, Henry Clinton – her boyfriend when she is home, greets her. Henry is 30-years-old and was taken under the wing of Atticus Finch, Jean Louise's attorney father, when Henry (Hank) was a child and he moved in across the street from the Finch home with his mother. Henry is not of Jean Louise's social standing. He wants her to marry him, she is not ready to marry and she doesn't know if she loves him or not. Henry's mother died when Henry was fourteen and since her funeral took up most of the money she had, Atticus secretly used his own money to raise Henry. Henry is now an attorney and set to take over Atticus' practice.

Jean Louise and Henry have an interesting relationship. He loves her, she is unsure. He is sweet, honest and devoted. She tries not to be exacerbating but it is in her nature and she has a habit of infuriating him, only she can also bring him back to endearment quickly.

Atticus' sister, Alexandra, has moved in to the Finch house to care for her brother, as a severe case of rheumatoid arthritis makes it difficult for him to get along. Henry, is Atticus' eyes, hands and legs at work and Alexandra is all of that at home. Alexandra reprimands, even condemns, Jean Louise for not being the kind of southern daughter she was raised to be, one of breeding, who stays home to care for her ailing father in his time of need; however, at the same time, Alexandra moves in and cares for Atticus so Jean Louise does not have to. Jean Louise reflects that when she is far away from her aunt she respects and values her, but when they are close together they are like oil and water – the old way of the Jim Crow south mixing with the new. From the moment Jean Louise and Atticus interact, she becomes Scout, the daughter who worships her father. This is important as it plays and imperative part of the overall story.

Jean Louise has a date with Hank her first night home, before which she and her aunt have a spat. Her aunt says that Jean Louise is too good for Henry, as he is trash and will always be trash. Aunt Alexandra says any good habits he conveys are the result of Atticus, but that Henry is just using Atticus for stature and that Henry wants everything that belongs to Atticus – implying the inclusion of Jean Louise.

Part I ends with Jean Louise thinking that she is closer to marrying Hank than she had ever been before.

Information Text Ti-In: Show clips of *I Love Lucy* and/or *Leave it to Beaver* that depict women in the 1950s.
Women in the 1950s Resources:
- http://www.pbs.org/wgbh/amex/pill/peopleevents/p_mrs.html
- http://www.eisenhower.archives.gov/research/online_documents/women_in_the_1950s.html
- http://www.colorado.edu/AmStudies/lewis/1025/women1950s.pdf
- http://mentalfloss.com/article/52108/7-tips-keeping-your-man-1950s

Name: _____ Date: _____

Go Set a Watchman Comprehension Quiz – Part I

1. Jean Louise Finch is heading home to Maycomb, Alabama from where?
    a. An all women's college in Georgia
    b. Finch Landing
    c. New York
    d. Monroeville, Alabama

2. Who greeted Jean Louise at the train station?
    a. Her father
    b. Aunt Alexandra
    c. Uncle Jack
    d. Henry Clinton

3. Calpurnia, the Finch family cook and care provider, ran off the place when?
    a. When Jean Louise went to college
    b. When Aunt Alexandra moved in
    c. When Jem died
    d. When Hank came into the picture

4. What does Aunt Alexandra think of Henry, Hank Clinton?
    a. She thinks he would make a fine husband for Jean Louise
    b. She thinks he is a great help to Atticus
    c. She thinks he is trash
    d. There is no indication of how she feels

5. Jean Louise believes that her aunt thinks every daughter in Maycomb should do her duty. What is *her* duty
    a. Return home and help take care of her father
    b. Go out into the world and become independent
    c. Marry a local and set up a home
    d. Go to teas with her aunt and be a proper Southern female

6. What sport does Jean Louise practice on the living room floor?
    a. Shuffleboard
    b. Golf
    c. Stretching
    d. Yoga

7. Summarize Part 1 in three sentences: _____
_____
_____
_____
_____

Name: _____ Date: _____

Questions for Critical Thinking – Part I

1. Analyze the following quote in the context of Part 1:
   "She was almost in love with him. No, that's impossible, she thought: either you are or you aren't. Love's the only thing in live that is unequivocal. There are different kinds of love, certainly, but it's a you-do or you-don't proposition with them all.

_____
_____
_____
_____

2. The theme of gender inequality runs throughout Part I of *Go Set a Watchman*. Support this statement in your own words, but be sure to use concrete evidence from the novel.

_____
_____
_____
_____
_____
_____
_____
_____

3. Describe Jean Louise's relationship to her Aunt Alexandra. Be sure to support your answer with evidence from the text.

_____
_____
_____
_____
_____
_____
_____
_____

Part II: Teacher Pages

Part II: Summary and Analysis

Scout and Hank go to dinner. The hotel restaurant has modernized since Scout's last visit and the only thing Scout likes about the upgrades is that the place no longer smells. The town of Maycomb is described as a place where, up until the Second World War, everyone was related. Maycomb is the manipulated center of the county. A man name Sinkfield, who had a tavern, apparently liquored up the surveyors and sent them back to the governor with more shine – some for them and some for the governor – after he cut from the map of Maycomb County here and added to it there to make his location the county seat. The town stayed the same for 150 years, but evidence of change now abounds. Maycomb is described as a former town of professionals with people coming from all over the county for the services of lawyers and doctors and dentists and the like.

Things in Maycomb began to change when *the boys* came back from World War II. For these returning soldiers, there was an urgency to make money and make up for lost time. Those returning altered their parent's houses, put up neon signs, built brick houses for themselves and named the streets.

After dinner, Jean Louise and Hank share a drink, hers light because apparently she can't hold her liquor and they drive to the river. The river is some distance away and Jean Louise dozes on the trip. Hank thinks about Atticus telling him not to push Jean Louise, because that makes her more stubborn than a team of mules. Hank considers himself Jean Louise's owner and thinks to himself: *"[h]e is her true owner, that was clear to him."* The theme of gender inequality is woven throughout the novel in the way the women act, in how they are treated, in how they are spoken to and in how they speak and Jean Louise's character is no exception. Women were fighting for equity in the 1950s, as well as African Americans, and this is evident throughout the story.

Hank's thoughts run on to Dill and he asks where their childhood friend is? Dill was the sometimes summertime neighbor of the Finches when he came to visit his great aunt, Miss Rachel. Jean Louise answers Italy and asks where they are. Ten more miles to go. Jean Louise observes that Hank never liked Dill. Hank admits he was jealous of him when they were young.

Time stops and Jean Louise is in a daydream, back to the dog days of August with her brother Jem and Dill playing Tom Swift, drinking lemonade and playing revival. Maycomb had three churches, Methodist, Baptist and Presbyterian and each summer there were joint revivals – against sin and things like Coca-Cola, picture shows, hunting on Sundays, women, drinking in public and drinking whiskey. The summer of which she was reminiscing was a Baptist hosted revival. The Finches are Methodist, but they, as well as most of Maycomb, attend all of the revivals. Reverend Moorhead was the preacher at the time and while the children could not really understand him, they were entertained by the whistle he made when he spoke, caused by a gap in his front teeth. When playing Baptist revival in their backyard, Jem decides to "baptize" Scout in a style they believe to be "Baptist" style. She strips naked so she doesn't get her clothes wet, Dill disappears and reappears dressed in a sheet. He is the Holy Ghost, until his great-aunt, Miss Rachel, appears to retrieve her best sheet and reprimand her great nephew. Through the struggle, Dill falls in the fish pond. All the while, Calpurnia, the Finch's black cook has been calling for the children and they have been ignoring her.

Miss Rachel marches Dill home. Jem and Scout decide to go in because it must be near dinnertime and they run right into Atticus, the Baptist Preacher and his wife – who have come to dinner. Atticus orders them to go to Calpurnia, through the back door. Jem realizes she is naked in front of the preacher. Calpurnia asks why ignored her calls. They lie and tell her they didn't hear her.

Calpurnia scrubs up Scout and dresses her in a pink dress and leather shoes. Scout and Jem sit quietly in the living room. At the dinnertime blessing, the Reverend's blessing includes a reprimand of the motherless children and their games. Scout feels terrible and the blessing apparently makes their father cry. He rises and excuses himself into the kitchen.

Calpurnia comes with a tray of food, while she was serving, Scout whispers to her, asking if Atticus was upset. Calpurnia answers that their father is on the back porch laughing.

Hank brings Jean Louise (Scout) out of her daydream, wondering where she was. They have arrived at Finch's Landing – her family's ancestral home by the river. It was the home of her great, great, great grandfather and a place of family reunions and good memories. It is the one place Jean Louise would return to and marry Hank. If she could stay at the Landing, she would stay in Maycomb. Hank tells her they are trespassing and then tells her the family sold the last of the Landing – the beautiful white house with sweeping porches and the little bit of land left is now gone.

She and Hank speak more of marriage. He tells her he wants to run for the legislature. Her father was in the legislature and was unopposed for a long time, when he decided to not run again, the "machine" took over his seat and now Hank believes it is time to take it back.

Scout tells Hank that Maycomb is the world and that when she is in New York she doesn't feel like she is out in the world, but when she comes home to Maycomb she does. Part II ends with Hank and Jean Louise pushing each other into the river and then driving home.

On the drive, a car speeds by them. Hank explains it is: *"A carload of negroes"* with *"…no licenses or insurance…"* – foreshadowing events to come. Once inside her house, she chooses a book and falls asleep in the bed in which she was born.

Resources:
- http://spartacus-educational.com/USAjimcrow.htm

Side Notes: Why the Title?

Harper Lee grew up in a Bible reading family and the title is from the King James Version.

Isaiah was a prophet in the Kingdom of Judah, between about 740 B.C. and 698 B.C. In this verse, he is prophesying about the fall of Babylon. The Babylon of immoral voices and hypocrisy. Somebody needs to be set as the watchman to identify what we need to do to get out of the mess.

Think: Atticus as the watchman
Think: Jean Louise as the watchman

http://www.al.com/living/index.ssf/2015/02/go_set_a_watchman_whats_the_bi.html

Name: _____ Date: _____

Go Set a Watchman Comprehension Quiz – Part II

1. Maycomb grew and sprawled out from its hub, which was?
    a. Sinkfield's Tavern
    b. Finch's Landing
    c. Wyatt Junction
    d. Maycomb proper

2. Jean Louise asks Hank: *"Don't you know how to catch a woman, honey?"* What does she say next...
    a. *"Make them feel helpless, especially when you know they can pick up a load of light'ud knots with no trouble."*
    b. *"Be strong and successful."*
    c. *"Charm them with you knowledge."*
    d. *"Be big and strong."*

3. *Henry drove up to the E-Light Eat Shop and honked the horn. "Give us two set-ups please, Bill..."* What was Hank ordering?
    a. Coke
    b. milk
    c. alcohol
    d. root beer

4. When Hank asks Jean Louise where their childhood friend Dill is, what does she respond?
    a. Paris
    b. London
    c. Italy
    d. New York

5. In the flashback, who strips naked for a pretend baptism?
    a. Dill
    b. Scout
    c. Hank
    d. Jem

6. Part II ends with Jean Louise:
    a. driving around with a carload of friends
    b. eating at the E-Light Eat Shop
    c. climbing into the bed she was born in and falling asleep
    d. thinking about her childhood friend Dill.

8. Summarize Part II in three sentences: _____
_____
_____
_____
_____

Name: _____ Date: _____

Informational Text Tie-In Analyzing Main Ideas RI.5, RI.6

Women were a major part of the American workforce during World War II, but when the soldiers returned to hometowns across the United States, women found themselves placed back into their *rightful* place in the home.

Then came the 1950s, with happy homemakers and the sprawl of the suburbs, with manicured lawns, teas in the South and powerful post-World War II propaganda encouraging women to stay home, get married, have babies and live the American Dream. Despite the best efforts of large persuasive advertising campaigns, women began to start the journey towards equal rights, attain higher education and seek true equality.

Picture the scenes you watched from *I Love Lucy*. While Ricky went out to work raging at the Copacabana, Lucy was left to take care of the home, cook and clean, take care of the family and follow the directions of her husband. She was often treated like a child. Women were definitely less than men.

When women did go to college it was often to hone their domestic skills or to obtain an MRS – aka find a husband. What is less studied or known is that in the 1950s female scholars began to emerge and take their place as college professors, but according to the New York Times in the 1950's women became college professors for the same reason they went to college – to find husbands.

When employed, the majority of women worked in nursing, teaching or typing and only 29% of the workforce was female – half of which were 35 and older.

What is the Main Idea?

With women returning to the workforce after being ousted at the end of World War II, and some women looking for academic opportunities that had little or nothing to do with finding a husband, the 1950s saw the rise of feminist to help women find equal footing. Women's rights organizations began chanting for equal pay for women, and women's magazines such as the Ladies' Home Journal encouraged women to take part in politics and political action and the tide began to turn.

Give Examples from the Text that Support the Main Idea?

Name: _____ Date: _____

Historical Document Analysis

This article was posted in Pictures from History https://twitter.com/HistoryInPics from the Times' New York Mirror and is reproduced under fair use license.
What is the main Idea from the clips?
_____
_____
_____
_____

What do the clips say about how society thought about women in the 1950s?
_____
_____
_____
_____

Compare the clips to Part I of *Go Set a Watchman*. Site evidence to either support or refute your argument.
_____
_____
_____
_____
_____
_____
_____
_____
_____

If a Woman Needs It, Should She Be Spanked?

[Today's question by Herman Martin, 125 Broad St., New York 4, N. Y.]

MIGUEL MATOS, Brooklyn, counterman: "Why not? If they don't know how to behave by the time they're adults, they should be treated like children and spanked. That ought to make them grow up in a hurry. If it doesn't at first, they'll soon get the idea."

FRANK DESIDERIO, Brooklyn, barber: "Yes, when they deserve it. As a barber, I've got a lot of faith in the hairbrush. I think there are certain cases when it is advisable. When it is, there's no reason why you shouldn't go right ahead and do it. I can't knock the idea. In my business, a man sets a lot of store by the results he can get with a hairbrush properly applied."

Name: _____ Date: _____

Compare Historical Document to Part II of *Go Set a Watchman*

Directions: Choose a quote from Part II that expresses the theme of gender inequality and compare and contrast it to the statement in the historical document from **Pictures From History**.

Part 1 quote: _____

_____

_____

_____

_____

| Watchman | Both | Document |

Name: _____ Date: _____

Quote Analysis of *Go Set a Watchman* – Making Inferences RL.1

Directions: Complete the foldable, cut it out and place it in your interactive notebook.

Remember: An inferences is the conclusion you reach based on evidence from the text and your own thoughts.

Behind Door Number 1
Quote from page: _____

Behind Door Number 2
My quote means...

Behind Door Number 3
My quote implies....

Behind Door Number 4
I know this because ...
Evidence and Details

Part III: Teacher Pages

Part III: Summary and Analysis

The morning after her visit to the Landing, Jean Louise is jolted from her sleep by Aunt Alexandra's calls and sharp accusations of swimming naked with Henry Clinton. Jean Louise strings her aunt along, not telling the older woman they were indeed clothed, until Atticus comes in and discovers his daughter's crunchy dress and slip – obviously in a state from a trip in a river. He tells her to stop torturing her aunt. Aunt Alexandra tells Jean Louise it doesn't matter; the town thinks it happened, so she, Aunt Alexandra will have to right the situation. The morning is Sunday and Aunt Alexandra will set all straight by the end of church.

Jean Louise comes out ready for church and Aunt Alexandra remarks that she has never seen her niece completely dressed in her life – as she is not wearing a hat. Jean Louise reflects that the only time she wore a hat was her brother's funeral. She reminisces about how she felt the need to wear one, so before the funeral she made Mr. Ginsberg open his store for her to choose one to wear. Jean Louise's reflections and flashbacks are imperative to the themes of the novel, as well as serve provide a window into the privilege that is taken for granted by one in Jean Louise's position, in the South, at that time.

Beloved Uncle Jack is waiting for them at church. Uncle Jack looks like Aunt Alexandra, except he is *spidery* and she is of *firmer proportions*. The reader learns that putting Uncle Jack through medical school was the reason Atticus didn't marry until he was forty, but that Jack paid his brother back and then some Uncle Jack is eccentric and absentminded with a sharp wit and an obsession with Victorian obscurities. Outwardly, he gives the appearance that he is a bit crazy, but he is *crazy like any fox ever born*.

The setting in church symbolizes the divide even within the same class. Jean Louise's father and uncle sit on the left side of the auditorium and she and her aunt sit on the right side of the auditorium. Symbolically right is good – alluding back to Tom Robinson's hand in the trial portion of *To Kill a Mockingbird*. The alignment of Jean Louise and Aunt Alexandra foreshadows a more thorough bond between the two and a greater appreciation, respect and acceptance of her niece than Alexandra lets on.

In church, Henry passes the collection plate and the music director sings the Doxology (a Doxology is a short hymn to praise God). Jean Louise can only remember one way this has ever been sung, only the music director, Herbert Jemson, has recently been to a church music camp and was influenced by folks from New Jersey and now sings it differently. Pulling rank, and symbolizing their position in the community, Jack Finch approaches the music director and brings him to admitting that the new way is wrong, northern and was only an experiment to see what people would do. Basically, it will never happen again.

Chapter 7, in Part III, is the first mention of the Supreme Court, and the *new* way to sing the hymn is a metaphor for the North imposing their ways on the South:

> Dr. Finch sat down in the front pew. He slung his arm across the back and moved his fingers meditatively. He looked up at Herbert.
> "Apparently," he said, "our brethren in the Northland are not content with merely the Supreme Court's activities. They are now trying to change our hymns on us."

Side Note: In the early 1950s the National Association for the Advancement of Colored People (NAACP) concentrated on bringing an end to segregation on buses and trains. In 1952 segregation on inter-state railways was declared unconstitutional by the Supreme Court. For some, this was not a matter of segregation but of an imposition on States' rights by the Federal Government.

This is the first sign we see of a Finch, outside of Alexandra, hinting at a position at odds with equality and it just brushes by on a few short pages. The interchange between Herbert and Dr. Finch ends with *"Don't worry sir"* uttered by Herbert. **Theme:** class structure.

Chapter 8 opens with post church normality in the Finch household. Atticus is reading the paper and Jean Louise is going to visit with her uncle, whom she finds amusing, engaging and highly intelligent – if not more than a bit eccentric. Henry comes in and picks Atticus up for a meeting. A meeting on Sunday? Yes.

Jean Louise sets about cleaning the living room and a business envelope catches her eye. On it is a drawing of an anthropophagous black person with *The Black Plague* written above it. She sits down in her father's chair, metaphorically by doing so she should be walking in his shoes, and reads the pamphlet.

Jean Louise questions her aunt about the pamphlet and Alexandra tells her it is something her father brought home from the Maycomb County Citizens' Council meeting – of which her father is on the board of directors and Henry is a member. Jean Louise is shocked. What she knows of citizen council meetings she has learned in New York newspapers.

Side Note Again: At the most basic level, Citizen's Councils were an associated network of organizations formed, mostly in the South, to oppose de-segregation.

Against her aunt's advise, Jean Louise goes to the courthouse and up to the *"Colored balcony"* from which she watched Tom Robinson's trial in *To Kill a Mockingbird*. Thus, she has come full circle. It was from here she proudly watched her father stand up for her convictions and continue is rise to icon or god-like status. Atticus Finch, the pinnacle and now it is the very spot from which he falls.

In the courtroom below, Jean Louise sees many of the men from Maycomb County – from trash to pillars. People who are her friends and relatives mixing with people they disrespect and even despise. Jean Louise witnesses her father introduce a man who spews toxic prejudicial and hateful words. Her mind whirls. Jean Louise cannot believe any of it is happening. As this man, Mr. O'Hanlon, spits out profane statements about mongrelizing the South, essential inferiority…kinky woolly heads, greasy smelly…she hears her father's voice in her head from *"…the warm comfortable past. 'Gentlemen if there's one slogan in this world I believe, it is this; equal rights for all, special privileges for none.'"*

Here is Chapter 8 we learn of another rape trial Atticus took – even though he did not like criminal law. Calpurnia brought an innocent young black man, charged with rape, to Atticus and he won an acquittal with a white jury. After the verdict, Atticus walked home and took a steaming bath – cleansing himself symbolically – and never realizing that two pair of eyes, like his own, were always upon him: Jean Louise.

Finally, Jean Louise can take no more. She is nauseated and stumbles out of the courtroom and out of the darkness of the courthouse into the blinding light of the steaming afternoon sun. It is so bright that it hurts her eyes – mirroring the pain of her broken heart after witnessing her father and the man she was contemplating marrying unveil a side she did not know existed – unraveling beliefs she did not know they harbored.

Jean Louise walks back to her old house, now an ice cream shop. She orders vanilla and goes to eat it in the backyard sans chinaberry tree and carhouse. The ground is awash with white gravel. She is dazed as the one human being who she trusted, fully and wholly, failed her, betrayed her, thus the world in which she existed shatters. Innocence is truly gone for Scout.

Chapter 9 opens with back story on Atticus. He is a man of integrity, humor and patience, who marries a woman fifteen years younger than he, has two children and at forty-eight is widowed. He raises his two small children with their *Negro cook* Calpurnia. Atticus Finch was always there for his children. He played with them and read to them – only he read to them what he was reading, history, bills being enacted into law, *True Detective Mysteries* – and by that shaped their views of the world.

The reader learns that after Jean Louise graduates high school, Atticus sent to a women's college in George and when she finished there he sent her to New York, or somewhere, to help her learn to get along in the world by herself. Jean Louise lived her life under the question *"What would Atticus do?"* and now all that has changed for her.

Back to reality, and the ice cream parlor, and Jean Louise finds a corner of the yard and vomits. She goes home and goes directly to bed. She will not go out with Henry that night.

Jean Louise is heart-broken and physically sick by the events of the day, by the realization that her insular world is not all she believed it to be and by the fact that her father is a different man than she had ever known. She has a defect that is coming to light – she is color blind in a world where color matters to the extreme.

Teacher Notes:

Name: _____ Date: _____

Go Set a Watchman Comprehension Quiz – Part III

1. At the beginning of Part III what does Aunt Alexandra accuse Jean Louise of?
    a. swimming with Henry
    b. swimming with her dress on with Henry
    c. swimming naked with Henry
    d. swimming at the Landing with Henry

2. At church, Atticus sits next to his brother. Who does Jean Louise sit next to?
    a. Scout
    b. Aunt Alexandra
    c. Uncle Jack
    d. Miss Rachel and Dill

3. What inspires the music director to change the way the congregation sings the Doxology?
    a. a conference he attended in New Jersey
    b. a conference he attended in Maycomb
    c. a music camp he attended in Alabama
    d. a music camp he attended in South Carolina

4. Fill in the blank: *"Apparently,"* he (Dr. Finch) said, *"apparently our brethren in the Northland are not content merely with the _____ activities. They are now trying to change our hymns on us."*
    a. Supreme Court's
    b. Methodist clergy
    c. prayer
    d. song selecting

5. Jean Louise finds a pamphlet that contains racially derogatory text and images. Aunt Alexandra tells her it belongs to whom?
    a. Atticus
    b. Jack
    c. Alexandra
    d. the reverend

6. What happened to cause Jean Louise to feel sick, her stomach shut, her feet clumsy and her body begin to tremble?
    a. she finds out that her father is a racist
    b. she finds out that the Citizens' Council wants to crack down on anyone not of their race
    c. Henry Clinton tells her he wants to marry her
    d. Henry Clinton tells her he doesn't want to marry her

Please answer the following on a separate piece of paper.

7. From the point of view of Jean Louise, describe the Citizen's Council Meeting.
8. Summarize Part III of *Go Set a Watchman* in ten sentences or less.

Name: _____ Date: _____

Support Your Assertions

At this point in the story, what do you think is the significance of Jean Louise's beliefs regarding Calpurnia and other African Americans? Defend your answers with evidence.

Significance:	
Evidence of Significance	
Evidence of Significance	
Evidence of Significance	
Conclusion:	

Active Reading for Universal Access: Making Inferences RL.1

Making an inference is as simple as reading between the lines. It is the same as drawing a conclusion based on what you have read added to your common sense.

Inference = what you read + common sense

You make inferences all of the time. Say you are in a car and you hear a loud crash and glass shattering. You didn't see what happened but you can guess, or infer, that there was a car crash of some kind.

When you read, you make inferences about plot and setting and characters all of the time.

Use the graphic organizer to make inferences about

Sample Character or Event: Scout comes home and for the first time her father does not greet her.	
Details from the Story: In Chapter 1, Scout is on the train thinking about her father greeting her. He always does; however, when she arrives she is greeted by Henry Clinton instead.	My Experiences: When something is out of the ordinary, I wonder why. What has changed? If someone usually meets me and they are supposed to but don't – I wonder if they are okay.
What I can infer: Something has changed with Atticus. He is either sick or injured. This will probably have some symbolic affect. Perhaps it foreshadows changes internal to him that are to come.	

Part III Making Inferences - CCSS RL.1

Your Turn: Select an event from Part III and make inferences about what will happen later in the story.

Passage from the Text:	
Details from the Story:	My Experiences:
What I can infer:	

Part IV Teacher Pages

Part IV: Summary and Analysis

When Scout was in the sixth grade, a school in another part of the county burned and many children came to her school while theirs was being reconstructed. The children where older – boys of nineteen and girls of sixteen – studying with her. Jean Louise took to the new students. They were nice and being a tomboy she played with the boys – and learned that their rough gentleness was easy to like. The big girls giggled a lot and kept to themselves.

All was great until one day Scout went home for dinner and started menstruating. When she returned to school, the big girls discovered her plight and she started to hang out with them when she was menstruating as it limited her activities. Jean Louise helped one older boy with his schoolwork, one day he walked her to class and told her he got a C minus in geography. She was proud. He was happy and he French-kissed her. She didn't think much of it really.

Later the older girls were talking about getting pregnant and when Scout revealed she didn't really know how pregnancy occurred, they described it as a French kiss and she silently suffered for almost a full year – waiting to disgrace her family with a baby. About three months into her depression, she found out that it took nine months to have a baby, so she began making a calendar. The date of her baby arriving was to fall in October, so she picked a dated in September to kill herself. When the day came, she climbed up a high water tower, Henry say her, went up to get her and dragged her home.

Calpurnia was finally able to persuade Jean Louise to tell her what was wrong and then proceeded to tell the child how babies really were born. Calpurnia showed love, compassion and motherly understanding. When Jem comes home, Jean Louise thinks he will tease her and she is mortified, but all he says is that she can always come to him if she ever has a problem.

Back to present, Jean Louise wakes up still in a daze, picks up her cigarettes, goes outside and ruminates on how she usually loves to stand and bask in the early morning air, taking in the mockingbirds' early service. The insertion of the mockingbirds here flicker brilliantly on the theme of innocence lost – this day – the day after the heart-wrenching discovery that her father is not the man she thought he was, not the man she made him to be – she can no longer tolerate innocence.

Jean Louise gets out the lawn mower; her aunt calls to reprimand her for mowing so early and tells her she must take her father to work. Jean Louise goes inside and cannot bare her father. The phone rings at breakfast. It is the Sheriff for Atticus, he tells Alexandra to have him call Hank. Jean Louise looks at her father, expecting to see differences but she does not. Hank comes and she is cold to him. They discover that Zeebo's boy, Calpurnia's great-grandson, was driving and hit a drunk man killing him. The black man needs Atticus to represent him.

Atticus agrees, Hank is confused, but Atticus explains that it is best to help the boy plead guilty and to handle it locally because the lawyers paid by the NAACP are standing around like *buzzards* waiting for things like this to happen. Jean Louise states that she thought the NAACP was forbidden to do business in Alabama. Atticus and Hank laugh at her. She leaves the room.

Before she takes her father to work, she goes to the grocery store and Mr. Fred gives her a Coke and gathers what is on Alexandra's list. Jean Louise has forgotten her money, but promises her father will pay when he comes to town – another sign of privilege. She returns home, gets her father, drops him off and goes to pay her respects to Calpurnia.

There are lots of people at Calpurnia's home: some dressed well, some in work clothes and some in their finest. They are nice, but stand-offish to Jean Louise and while Calpurnia agrees to see Jean Louise, the former mother figure is cold and uses a polite tone once only reserved for white strangers. Scout is crushed because she has always considered Cal family. The old woman has changed. Jean Louise is shocked. This is the woman who raised her, who mourned Jem, who loved her and worshipped her brother.

Jean Louise is taken aback. Before she leaves she asks if Calpurnia hates them. After a long while, Calpurnia shakes her head.

Teacher Notes:

Name: _____ Date: _____

Go Set a Watchman **Comprehension Quiz – Part IV**

1. Part IV opens with a flashback and we learn that students from Old Sarum will be attending school with Jean Louise and Jem because of a fire at the Old Sarum school site. What is different about the students from Old Sarum?
    a. they are old for their grades
    b. they are smart
    c. they ride to school in a yellow bus
    d. they play with Jean Louise, Scout

2. What does Albert, a boy from Old Sarum, do to cause Jean Louise to believe she is pregnant?
    a. he French kisses her
    b. he tackles her
    c. he hugs her
    d. he kisses her

3. Who rescues Jean Louise from the tower?
    a. Albert
    b. Calpurnia
    c. Jem
    d. Henry

4. In the morning, what does Jean Louise usually take great pleasure in listening too, but can't this morning after she witnesses her father at the Citizen's Council meeting?
    a. music
    b. mockingbirds
    c. the breeze in the trees
    d. crickets

5. Who needs the services of either Atticus or Henry?
    a. Calpurnia's boy Zeebo
    b. Aunt Alexandra's boy Zeebo
    c. Zeebo the fireman
    d. no one

6. Why does Atticus tell Henry they have to take the case?
    a. to keep the NRA away
    b. to help the Citizen's Council
    c. to keep the NAACP away
    d. because it is the proper thing to do

7. On a separate piece of paper, please describe Jean Louise's visit with Calpurnia.

> **Point of view** is the "writer's voice". To determine the point of view ask yourself: who is telling the story?

Name: _____ **Date:** _____

Part IV: *Go Set a Watchman: Point of View*

Third Person Point of View: Here the narrator does not participate in the action of the story as one of the characters, but lets us know exactly how the characters feel. We learn about the characters through this outside voice *Go Set a Watchman* is written in *third person point of view*.

First Person Point of View: In the first person point of view, the narrator does participate in the action of the story. When reading stories in the first person, we need to realize that what the narrator is recounting might not be the objective truth. We should question the trustworthiness of the accounting.

Choose a character from this chapter and re-write a scene using the **First Person Point of View**.
Character: _____

_____
_____
_____
_____
_____
_____
_____
_____
_____
_____
_____
_____
_____
_____
_____
_____
_____

Part V: Teacher Pages

Part V: Summary and Analysis

At home, Jean Louise realizes it is the day for her tea and the guests will arrive at 10:30. She is in no mood, but she is a Southern lady and Alexandra has already arranged it all. The *magpies* arrive promptly. They are a mix of young marrieds, young mothers, young non-married rather undesirables and thirty-something marrieds. Alexandra tries to make small talk, but she really has nothing in common with these women. The talk turns to the NAACP and while the others are blabbing along, the Declaration of Independence comes into Jean Louise's thoughts, but it is thwarted to fit the current situation:

> *Conceived in mistrust, and dedicated to the proposition that all men are created evil... When in the course of human events it becomes necessary for one people to dissolve the political bands, which have connected them with another – they are Communists.*

The young women of Maycomb ask about New York and Jean Louise describes being surrounded by black people only she doesn't even notice. They can't believe it and she herself realizes she is not only color blind, but blind to what is in people's hearts – just as Atticus is blind in one eye – all symbolic of not seeing the truth – not seeing the injustice – shrouded in ignorance or at least in darkness.

Jean Louise's mind wonders to the preacher setting a watchman in church the previous day. Jean Louise thinks to herself that she needs a watchman *"...lead me around and declare what he seeth every hour on the hour. I need a watchman to tell me this is what a man says but this is what he means, to draw a line down the middle and say here is this justice and there is that justice and make me understand the difference. I need a watchman to go forth and proclaim to them all that twenty-six years is too long to play a joke on anybody, no matter how funny it is."*

She must go see Uncle Jack, but going to her uncle's is like going down the rabbit hole. Chapter 14 is reminiscent of the Mad Hatter's Tea Party. Dr. Finch, aka Uncle Jack, talks about the South being like a little feudal England in its heritage and social structure and then he talks about the civil war being a rag-tag group of individuals who walked off their farms and walked to war. Uncle Jack asks if Jean Louise knew why the Civil War was fought. She answers *"...slaves and tariffs and things..."*.

He points out that: *"...not more than five per cent of the South's population ever saw a slave, much less owned one. Now, something must have irritated that last ninety-five percent."* Uncle Jack asks if it ever occurred to Jean Louise that the South was really its own entity, its own nation within a nation. Yes, Southern society was highly paradoxical and inequities existed to the extreme, but they were joined by their individual identities and they fought to preserve those identities – is he referring to States' Rights vs. civil rights? Have students decide.

Jean Louise points out that the Civil War had been over for about 100 years and Uncle Jack retorts that the only thing Reconstruction brought, the only political change, was that there was no more slavery. Plus, he counters; now the there was a new *breed of white men* in open competition with black people. For years these white men, as dirty and as hard and as poor and with as little breeding as slaves, were better than the black man because they were not slaves. That divide has changed.

Uncle Jack thinks aloud, hoping that this new Reconstruction will be comparatively bloodless. Then he beings talking about the duties of the government changing and how it now protects one from old age, as an example, because the government does not trust people to protect themselves. The tenant farmers have gone, but the tenant farmers of her generation are the factory workings in the little white houses on the other side of the town. These people are under the thumb of the government, which lends them money to build their houses and gives them a free education and unemployment if they lose their jobs. Jean Louise calls him cynical, but he says it isn't cynicism it is a *"mistrust of paternalism and government in large doses…"*

Then he states it, what he and Atticus are afraid of, a big and overreaching government.

The novel is set around 1952, when the Supreme Court began to overturn the Black Codes, the Jim Crow Laws, the separate is equal doctrine – when segregation on inter-state railroads was declared unconstitutional – Atticus and Uncle Jack thought the Federal Government had reached too far. Some saw this as a violation of States' Rights. Uncle Jack is putting himself and Atticus in the States' Right camp as previously discussed.

> On page 198 of the first edition Uncle Jake states: *"The only thing I'm afraid of about this country is that its government will someday become so monstrous that the smallest person in it will be trampled underfoot, and then it wouldn't be worth living in. The only thing in America that is still unique in this tired world is that a man can go as far as his brains will take him or he can go to hell if he wants to, but it won't be that way much longer."*

The only real duties of the government, in the opinion of Uncle Jack, should be to prevent crime, preserve contracts and perhaps provide for the common defense.

Jean Louise did not understand the correlation between what Uncle Jack said and the fact that relations between white and black people where worse than at any time in her life. Uncle Jack compares the current situation with the messiness of birth and states the South was in its last agonizing birth pain.

Jean Louise is indignant. Uncle Jack says he can't and won't stop what she should do and he mentions a Robert Browning Poem *Childe Roland*. Part of the poem is also the last line in King Lear. Part V ends with Uncle Jack picking up the telephone.

Childe Roland: The poem is about the mid-nineteenth century urbanization of the once rural England. A change brought about by the Industrial Revolution. With the urbanization came crime, poverty and a sense of freedom mixed with a sense of insecurity.

Name: _____ Date: _____

Go Set a Watchman Comprehension Quiz – Part V

1. Why is Aunt Alexandra upset when she learns Jean Louise went to see Calpurnia, the Finches' old cook?
    a. Because Calpurnia needs her father's help
    b. Because no one goes to see the *"negroes anymore"*
    c. Because Zeebo was there
    d. Because she went without her father or Hank

2. What social event does Jean Louise attend at her own house that she has little patience for?
    a. A dinner party
    b. A citizens' council meeting
    c. A tea arranged by her aunt in her honor
    d. A lunch for her friends

3. To try and sort things out, who does Jean Louise go visit?
    a. Uncle Jack
    b. Atticus
    c. Henry Clinton
    d. Jem

4. Uncle Jack tells her: *"You're making a bad mistake if you think your daddy's dedicated to keeping the Negroes in their places?"* What does Uncle Jack imply her father is really after?
    a. States' Rights
    b. Slavery
    c. What was incidental in the Civil War is incidental here
    d. Racism

5. According to Uncle Jack, what was the only permanent political change of Reconstruction?
    a. Equal rights
    b. The solidification of States' Rights
    c. No more slavery
    d. Selective slavery

6. As Part V ends, Uncle Jack goes into the kitchen and…
    a. Has a cup of coffee
    b. Has a cup of tea
    c. Picks up the telephone
    d. Becomes frustrated with his niece

On a separate piece of paper…

7. Summarize Part V in the context of the theme of co-existence of good and evil.
8. Use no more than five sentences to retell Uncle Jack's view of the actions of his brother Atticus Finch.

Part VI: Teacher Notes

Part VI: Summary and Analysis

Jean Louise goes back to the ice cream parlor and daydreams about a date with Hank, a school dance, where Hank rescued her twice and she begins to fall in love with him – but then not.

Jean Louise is upset that she no longer fits into her family and she goes to see her father. She meets Hank along the way, they go to the café, and she tells him she will never marry him. She brings up the citizens' council. He explains that the meetings aren't all bad and that even the Klan can be okay. Then he tells her that her father went to a Klan meeting once upon a time. She tells him that she can't live in Maycomb and she can't live with a hypocrite. Her father speaks behind her stating: *"Hypocrites have just as much right to live in this world as anybody."*

She has it out with her father. At first Atticus says it is a States' Rights issue that bothers him and that there are two reasons he was at the meeting: *The Federal Government and the NAACP*. He then asks his daughter's first reaction to the Supreme Court decision – Brown v. Board of Education.

Jean Louise tells her father that she agrees it was a horrible decision because it steps all over the Tenth Amendment, which grants States' Rights. They agree that the Court is extinguishing the Constitution and this is bad, but Jean Louise believes black people deserve a chance, as they are human beings. Atticus calls them backwards. He does not think black people are ready to be full citizens and it would be horrible for them to take office. He fully believes that full citizenship should be earned – a true Jeffersonian Democrat. Like Jefferson, does Atticus believe that *earning* citizenship means one is white and male? Hinting at the theme of gender inequality as well.

Again, Jean Louise agrees with her father that the NAACP is not a good thing, but that is where the agreement ends. The argument ensues and Jean Louise tells her father that he is a horrible person, that he betrayed her and that he was not better than Hitler.

Atticus says *that'll do* and states that he loves her. Jean Louise storms out of the office -- intent on never seeing her father or Maycomb ever again.

Reminder: *Brown v. Board of Education was actually the name given to five separate cases that were heard by the U.S. Supreme Court concerning segregation in public schools. These cases were* Brown v. Board of Education of Topeka, Briggs v. Elliot, Davis v. Board of Education of Prince Edward County (VA.), Boiling v. Sharpe, *and* Gebhart. *While the facts of each case are different, the main issue in each was the constitutionality of state-sponsored segregation in public schools – by ruling for "Brown" – States' Rights, via the Tenth Amendment would be trampled on.*

When the cases came before the Supreme Court in 1952, the Court consolidated all five cases under the name of Brown v. Board of Education. Thurgood Marshall personally argued the case before the Court. Although he raised a variety of legal issues on appeal, the most common one was that separate school systems for blacks and whites were inherently unequal, and thus violate the "equal protection clause" of the Fourteenth Amendment to the

U.S. Constitution. Furthermore, relying on sociological tests, he also argued that segregated school systems made black children feel inferior to white children, and thus such a system should not be legally allowed.

Meeting to decide the case, the Justices of the Supreme Court realized that they were deeply divided over the issues raised. While most wanted to reverse Plessy v. Ferguson and declare segregation in public schools unconstitutional, they had various reasons for doing so. Unable to come to a solution by June 1953 (the end of the Court's 1952-1953 term), the Court decided to rehear the case in December 1953. During the intervening months, however, Chief Justice Fred Vinson died and was replaced by Earl Warren of California. After the case was reheard in 1953, Chief Justice Warren was able to do something that his predecessor had not—get all of the Justices to agree to support a unanimous decision declaring segregation in public schools unconstitutional. In May 1954, Earl Warren delivered the opinion of the Court, stating that "We conclude that in the field of public education the doctrine of 'separate but equal' has no place. Separate educational facilities are inherently unequal. . ."

Resources:
- http://law2.umkc.edu/faculty/projects/ftrials/conlaw/sepbutequal.htm
- http://law2.umkc.edu/faculty/projects/ftrials/conlaw/RoadtoBrown.html
- http://law2.umkc.edu/faculty/projects/ftrials/conlaw/RoadtoBrown.html
- http://www.ourdocuments.gov/doc.php?flash=true&doc=87

Name: _____ Date: _____

Go Set a Watchman Close Reading – Part VI

1. In the flashback that opens Chapter 15, who accompanies Jean Louise to the school dance.
    a. Jem, as is the tradition
    b. Dill, her old friend from his summers with Miss Rachel
    c. Henry Clinton
    d. Atticus

2. Who helps Jean Louise learn to dance?
    a. Jem
    b. Atticus
    c. Uncle Jack
    d. Dill

3. What does Jean Louise wear that causes controversy at school the next day?
    a. Falsies
    b. Heels
    c. Spiked heels
    d. a hair bandana

4. Henry tells Jean Louise that her father attended what kind of meeting forty years ago?
    a. A Citizens' Council
    b. A woman's tea
    c. A Klan meeting
    d. An NAACP meeting

5. When Jean Louise is arguing with her father, what is the one thing he says is higher than the Supreme Court in this land?
    a. Congress
    b. The president
    c. The Constitution
    d. The governments of the states

6. What is the last thing Atticus says to Jean Louise before she storms out of his office?
    a. I love you
    b. That'll do
    c. You are right
    d. Go home and pack your bags

On a separate piece of paper…

7. Summarize and analyze the confrontation between Jean Louise and Atticus.
8. Who is portrayed as a bigger racist Henry or Atticus? Support your answer with details from

Name: _____ Date: _____

Close Read: Chapter 17

Answer the following questions on a separate piece of paper

First Read: Understanding the Basics:

1. What is the main idea of the text?
2. Summarize Chapter 17.
3. In your summary, circle the words or passages that jump out at you.
4. Write down any questions you have.

Second Read: Digging Deep

1. What text structures and text features were used?
2. What is the author's purpose?
3. How do you feel when you read the chapter?
4. Why did the author use particular words, nuances and phrases?

Third Read: Putting it All Together

1. What do you infer from the text?
2. How does this chapter relate to the other chapters in *Go Set a Watchman*?
3. List three key points from Chapter 17.
4. Tell how you know they are key points.

Quoting the Text:

1. Choose what you feel is the most important passage. Rewrite it, tell why you feel it is important and discuss what theme it relates to.

Teacher Pages: Part VII

Part VII: Summary and Analysis

Jean Louise is upset, but then she knew she could never win an argument against her father. She is leaving. She throws her suitcase on the bed. Her aunt tries to stop her and Jean Louise is hateful. Jean Louise starts to call Aunt Alexandra a *"...pompous, narrow-minded old..."* only she catches herself because she sees her aunt cry for the first time. Jean Louise apologizes and her Southern aunt acts with dignity and tells her niece not to worry about.

Jean Louise kisses her aunt's cheek and tells her that she, herself, is not much of a lady, but her aunt retorts: *"You're mistaken, Jean Louise, if you think you're no lady," said Alexandra. She wiped her eyes. "But you are right peculiar sometimes."*

As Jean Louise is packing the car, her uncle comes to stop her. She is crazed and won't listen; she is on a runner so he backhands her and almost knocks her out. They go inside, he fixes her up and he asks his sister for some of her whiskey, she denies having any, he tells her to get the one she uses for her fruitcakes and she does. Jack makes Jean Louise drink it and she begins to feel better.

Uncle Jack says that Atticus called and told him everything. He says *"every man's watchman is his conscience"* and that it is important for her to realize that her watchman is her own, not anyone else's, not even her father's. He also tells her that she is the bigot because she won't listen with an open mind.

They talk about Jean Louise being color blind, unable to see race. They further discuss interracial marriage and oddly she says she would never do that. She asks why he cares so much and he says that he was in love with her mother and that she, Jean Louise, and Jem are like his own children.

Jean Louise goes to pick up Atticus from work. He tells her he is proud she held *"...her ground for what she thought was right."* He says that it is imperative to have both sides. Jean Louise tells her father that she loves him, she gets into the car – this time she does not bump her head. Very symbolic.

Resources:
- Citizens' Councils: http://www.encyclopediaofalabama.org/article/h-3618
- Harper Lee: http://www.harperlee.com/bio.htm
- This is a great article from *The Atlantic* but copy and paste it for students into a document format as it has ads and links that may not necessarily. It is a look into the to Atticuses (Atticui?)
  http://www.theatlantic.com/entertainment/archive/2015/07/his-name-was-atticus/398600/

Name: _____ Date: _____

Go Set a Watchman End of Novel Exam

Answer true or false.

1. _____ Jean Louise Finch lives in Maycomb Alabama.
2. _____ Henry and Atticus are members of the Citizens' Council
3. _____ The house Jean Louise grew up in is a bakery
4. _____ Calpurnia is cold to Jean Louise
5. _____ Aunt Alexandra throws a tea for Henry
6. _____ Henry and Jean Louise are childhood friends
7. _____ Atticus is worried about the NAACP
8. _____ Jean Louise bumps her head getting into the car
9. _____ Jean Louise thinks hugging got her pregnant
10. _____ Finch Landing had recently been sold
11. _____ Jean Louise hates going down to the river
12. _____ Atticus never tells his children he loves them
13. _____ Jean Louise's brother is dead
14. _____ Jean Louise can't wait to marry Hank
15. _____ Atticus picks Jean Louise up at the airport
16. _____ Atticus picks Jean Louise up at the train station
17. _____ Jean Louise watches part of the meeting from the colored balcony
18. _____ Jean Louise learns her father was a Grand Dragon in the KKK
19. _____ The novel is set in Maycomb, Alabama
20. _____ Jean Louise's uncle is a doctor

21. Analyze the ending of the novel through the lens of the theme of racial inequality. _____

_____

_____

_____

_____

_____

_____

22. Summarize the flashback when Henry Clinton rescues Jean Louise from the tower. _____

_____

_____

_____

_____

_____

_____

23. Compare and contrast Atticus and Henry Clinton: _____

_____

_____

_____

_____

_____

_____

24. Write a critique of *Go Set a Watchman* using at least three details from the novel. _____

25. Discuss what Atticus means when he says: *"The Negroes down here are still in their childhood as a people."* Include whether you think it is a racist statement or not. Defend your answer with evidence from the text.

_____
_____
_____
_____
_____
_____
_____
_____
_____

26. Aunt Alexandra disproves of Jean Louise when she wears –
    a) a kitten sweater
    b) high heels
    c) pants
    d) falsies

27. What does Uncle Jack do to get Jean Louise's attention when she is getting ready to leave for New York?
    a) Strikes her
    b) Gives her a drink
    c) Carries her bag to the car
    d) Yells at her

28. Who is described as "trash" by Aunt Alexandra?
    a) Henry
    b) Calpurnia
    c) Jean Louise
    d) Atticus

29. What ailment does Atticus has that restricts his activity.
    a) Arthritis
    b) Dementia
    c) He was hit by a car and has trouble walking
    d) Sleep apnea

30. Who is Jean Louise's brother?
    a) Jem
    b) Dill
    c) Henry
    d) Hank

Assignments

Name: _____ Date: _____

The Character and Theme Link (CCSS RL.2)

Choose four characters, link each to one to a theme of *Go Set a Watchman*, and site examples of this link through the character's actions, lack of actions, statements, decisions and/or quotes.

Character	Theme	Example
		Page number _____
		Page number _____
		Page number _____
		Page number _____

Name: _____ Date: _____

Character Analysis: How Jean Louise Sees Herself/ How Others See Jean Louise (CCSS RL.3)

How Scout Sees Herself	How do you see the Scout?	How Others Sees Scout

Name: _____ Date: _____

Impact of Author's Choice's CCSS RL.3

Write the character traits in the arrows. In the middle box, tell how specific events related to each individual, develop and join the characters over the course of the novel.

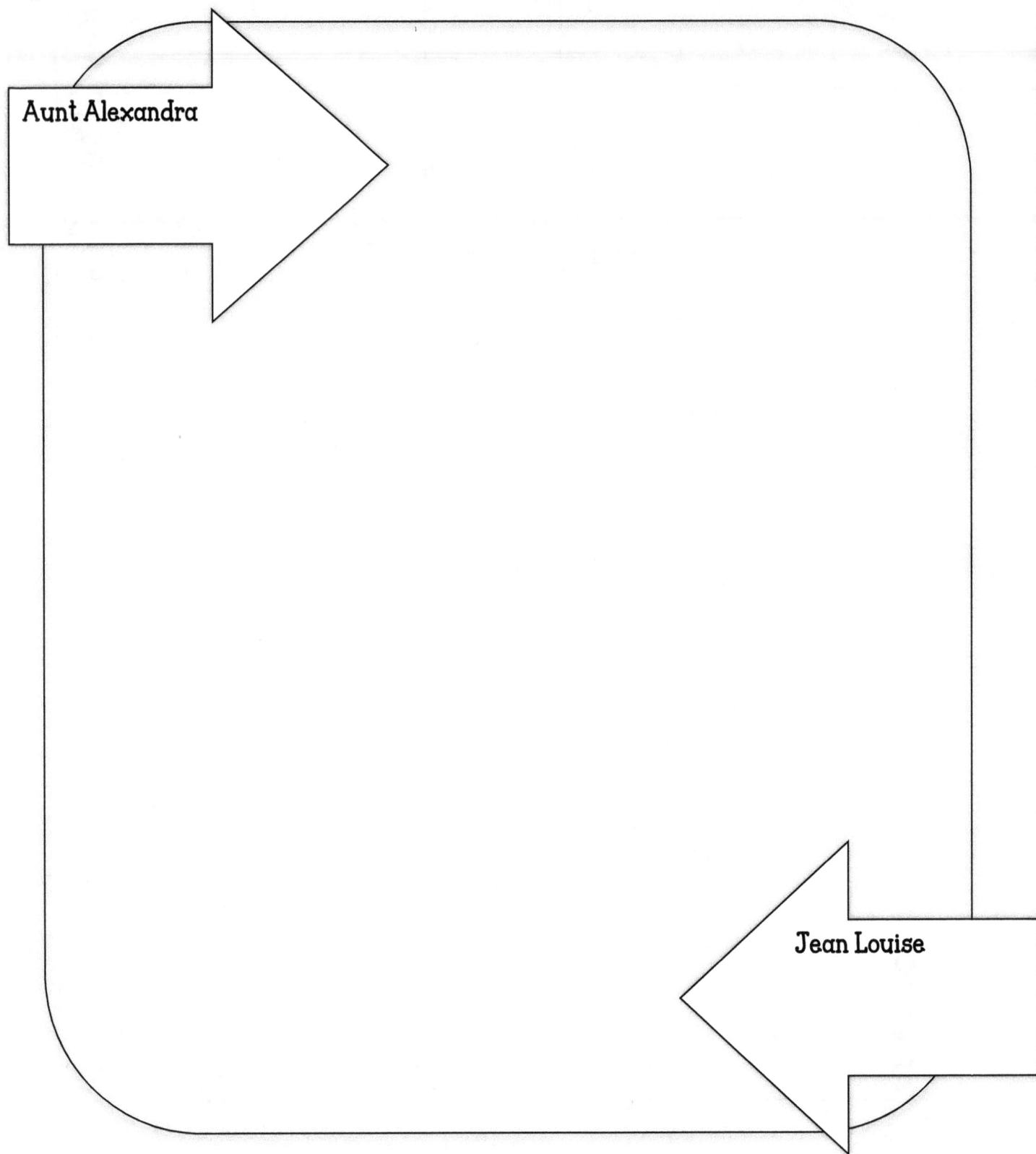

Name: _____ Date: _____

Plot Development - CCSS RL3 - Henry's Contributions

Main Event 2
Discuss how Henry's action contribute to the advancement of the plot:

Main Event 3
Discuss how Henry's action contribute to the advancement of the plot:

Main Event 1
Discuss how Henry's action contribute to the development of the plot:

Main Event 4
Discuss how Henry's action contribute to the resolution of the plot:

Start

Name: _____ Date: _____

Plot Development – CCSS RL3 – _____'s Contributions

Main Event 2
Discuss how the character's action contribute to the advancement of the plot:

Main Event 3
Discuss how the character's action contribute to the advancement of the plot:

Main Event 1
Discuss how the character's action contribute to the development of the plot:

Main Event 4
Discuss how the character's action contribute to the resolution of the plot:

Start

Name: _____ Date: _____

Plot Development - CCSS RL3 - The Setting's Contributions

Main Event 2
Discuss how the setting contributes to the advancement of the plot:

Main Event 3
Discuss how the setting contributes to the advancement of the plot:

Main Event 1
Discuss how the setting contributes to the development of the plot:

Main Event 4
Discuss how the setting contributes to the resolution of the plot:

Start

Name: _____ Date: _____

Elements of Part 1: *Go Set a Watchman* CCSS RL.3

	How Jean Louise is Shaped by the Story	How the Plot is Shaped by the Story
Setting	_____ _____ _____ _____	_____ _____ _____ _____
Order Of Events	_____ _____ _____ _____	_____ _____ _____ _____
Point Of View	_____ _____ _____ _____	_____ _____ _____ _____
Rising Action	_____ _____ _____ _____	_____ _____ _____ _____
Conflict	_____ _____ _____ _____	_____ _____ _____ _____

Name: _____ Date: _____

Dialogue Dissection - CCSS RL.3

Choose quotes from GSAW that propel the action, reveal aspects of a character and provoke a decision.

Propels the action of the novel	Quote:	Page #
	How does it propel the action	
Reveals aspects of a character	Quote:	Page #
	What does the quote reveal about _____?	
Provokes a decision	Quote:	Page #
	What decision is provoked?	

Name: _____ Date: _____

Word Choices – Connotative Meanings -- CCSS RL.4

Connotation refers to a meaning implied by a word apart from its literal meaning. Words carry cultural and emotional associations or meanings in addition to their literal meanings. In the spaces below, analyze the author's word choices.

Examples of Connotative Meanings in *Go Set a Watchman*	
Passage or quote from GSAW	
Literal meaning	
Connotative meaning – what emotion does it evoke?	
How does the passage or quote help to set the tone	
How does the passage or quote influence the overall meaning of the section	

Examples of Connotative Meanings in *Go Set a Watchman*	
Passage or quote from GSAW	
Literal meaning	
Connotative meaning – what emotion does it evoke?	
How does the passage or quote help to set the tone	
How does the passage or quote influence the overall meaning of the section	

Name: _____ Date: _____

Structure – Foreshadowing and Flashbacks -- CCSS RL.5

How did the author incorporate foreshadowing and how did the foreshadowing enhance the story?

How did the author incorporate flashbacks and how did the flashbacks enhance the story?

Socratic Discussion/Seminar Instructions

Common Core Anchor Standards Addressed: R1, R2, R5, W1, W9, SL1 and SL4

A Socratic Seminar is a structured discussion that allows students to engage and disagree in a way that is polite, focused and respectful. This activity enables students to think critically about texts and build confidence in their ideas and thought processes.

Students begin Socratic Seminars with a list of teacher (or student, depending upon the level) generated questions that help the group think critically about the text they are reading. Students pose questions to the group and take turns speaking and listening to each other's thoughts and ideas. All members of the discussion share learning as students work together to gain a deeper understanding of the text – as they extend, clarify and challenge themselves and each other.

Hint: Before you begin this activity, develop a signal to politely stop any student who may be dominating the conversation.

Students should complete a Seminar Template so they truly understand the text and their argument. A blank template immediately follows these instructions. This work may be done individually, in groups or as a whole class activity. If students are remedial or need extra help – working as a class, especially through the first few Socratic Discussions/Seminars – is extremely helpful.

1. Break into groups and circle up – or circle up one group with leftover students circled around the discussion group. The outer circle will act as scribes.

2. Establish and/or discuss the rules and norms of the discussion.

3. Review the purpose of the activity and your expectations. Model how students should participate and behave.

4. Select a discussion leader.

5. Set a time limit: 30 to 40 minutes is sufficient.

6. Begin the discussion.

7. Debrief: include discussing the groups strengths and weaknesses.

Helpful Hints: If your class is large, divide students into two circles, one inner and one outer. Leave one chair in the inner circle empty. This is the "roving seat." Students who are in the inner circle are active discussion members. Students in the outer circle can pop in and contribute. If it is not the first time you are doing this activity – you may actually have two seminars going at the same time. Twenty students is about the limit for active participation to be effective for all students; however, students are more engaged if group size is closer to twelve.

It is imperative to stress that students must reference the text often and that thinking and analyzing out of the box are essential – and encouraged – for this activity. Teachers should stay out of the conversation, but guide if necessary.

Name: _____ Date: _____ # _____

Go Set a Watchman
Socratic Seminar

Site two main ideas or claims from the novel to support your argument as it relates to the question.

1. _____
_____
_____
_____
_____
_____
_____
_____page:

2. _____
_____
_____
_____
_____
_____
_____
_____page:

List examples SUPPORTING your argument:

List examples COUNTERING your argument:

Socratic Seminar: Participant Rubric

Participant's name: _____ Date: _____

	4	3	2	1
Participant offers solid analysis, without prompting, to move the conversation forward.				
Participant, through his or her comments, demonstrates a depth of understanding of the text.				
Participant, through his or comments, demonstrates a depth of understanding for the question.				
Participant, through his or her comments, demonstrates he or she has actively listened to other participants.				
Participant offers clarification and follow-up that extends the conversation.				
Participant's remarks and comments refer to specific parts of the text.				
Participant is polite and respectful.				

Teacher comments: _____
_____
_____
_____
_____
_____

Student comments: _____
_____
_____
_____
_____
_____

Prompt Title: _____

Go Set a Watchman Interactive Notebook Universal Access

These Graphic Organizers and assignments are less challenging and ideal for differentiation or English Language Learner universal access. They can be used as worksheets or cut and pasted into student notebooks or interactive notebooks.

Go Set a Watchman

By Harper Lee #67

Cover Design by: _____

Design and draw your own book cover

Name: _____ # _____

Critical Thinking Questions- #68

How does Atticus show fondness for Jean Louise?
_____
_____
_____
_____

What would you do as Jean Louise?
_____
_____
_____
_____
_____

Compare Hank's views of race to Jean Louise's
_____
_____
_____
_____
_____
_____

Discuss how the author portrays Aunt Alexandra.
_____
_____
_____

Describe one way Jean Louise changes over the course of the novel?

Name: _____ # _____

About: Go Set a Watchman
In My Opinion… #69

What is your favorite part of the story? _____
_____
_____
_____

Details why…
1. _____
_____
_____

2. _____
_____
_____

Who is your favorite character? _____
_____

Details why…
1. _____
_____
_____

2. _____
_____
_____

What is the main problem or conflict in the story? _____
_____

Details…
1. _____
_____
_____

2. _____
_____
_____

Name: _____ #: _____

Go Set a Watchman
Constructed Response Questions - #69

Answer the following questions using complete sentences.

1. Describe the title in detail? _____
_____
_____
_____
_____
_____
_____
_____
_____

2. Use details to describe the one theme? _____
_____
_____
_____
_____

3. Describe Atticus in relation to the other characters in the novel. _____
_____
_____
_____
_____

4. Describe Ewell in relation to the other characters in the novel: _____
_____
_____
_____

Name: _____ #: _____

Story Connectors
Go Set a Watchman- #70

In the beginning _____
_____
_____
_____

After that _____
_____
_____
_____

Later _____
_____
_____
_____

Just when _____
_____
_____
_____

At the end _____
_____
_____
_____

Name: _____ #: _____

Character Analysis- #71

Character	Write three Character Traits for Each
Jean Louise	
Aunt Alexandra	
Uncle Jack	

Name: _____ #: _____

Jean Louise Character Conflicts – #72

Character Conflicts: A problem or struggle between two people, things or ideas.

What conflict developed as a result of Jean Louise's actions?
_____
_____
_____
_____
_____

How would you represent the actions of this conflict using the elements of the graphic novel? Draw it below.

Name: _____ #: _____

Sentence Sorting - #73

Cut the sentence strips below and arrange them in the order they occur in the story

Go Set a Watchman

1) Jean Louise sat in the balcony of the courthouse and watched her father and Henry in disbelief.

2) Jean Louise was expecting to see her father at the train Station, but it was henry Clinton who picked her up

3) Aunt Alexandra comes to live with the Finch's in Maycomb to give them a feminine influence. She is prim and proper and mortified that the children are allowed to go back to the courtroom to hear the verdict.

4) They drove the distance to Finch's Landing.

5) Atticus and Dr. Finch sat on the left and Jean Louise and her Aunt Alexandra sat on the right. They listened to the sermon and when it was time to sing the Doxology – the music director mixed it up. Dr. Finch did not like the new version and made it known.

6) Jean Louise picked up her father and when she got into the car, this time she was careful not to bump her head.

7) The ice cream parlor stood where her house used to be. She sat in the back on the white gravel and grew sicker and sicker – retreating into a corner and throwing up.

Sentence Sorting to Essay Writing Enrichment-#74

From Sentence Sorting to Essay Writing

GOAL: To gain a better understanding of what you read through reading and writing. To have an outline ready to go for an English/Language Arts writing assignment.

Directions:

Copy the template on the next page onto a transparency or use the computer generated sheet on a projector or document camera etc. Copy one blackline master per student.
Do a sample on the board and demonstrate the entire activity to the class – discuss the order of the sentence strips and copy them.
Check for understanding using think, speak and do strategies as you and your students write the essay together.
Review the sentence sorting activity as a group.
Work a modified scrip from the one herein to move from sentence sorting to essay writing.

Extension Assignment:

Have students choose a concept idea from the story.
Have students us the story to write their own sentence strips.
Re-pair up students with different partners and have them work self-created sentence strips.
Hand out another template and help students move from sentence strips to essay writing on their own.
For limited English proficient students and students who need extra help – you may want to do the assignment together – you on the board taking suggestions and them writing it down on their paper. Test and check as you help them to individualize their worksheet as you all move along together.

Hint to Motivate: Copy the template onto paper, laminate and have students use dry erase markers to construct their essays. When the rough draft is complete, have students peer edit and then copy their essays onto notebook paper. This saves time… helps with the editing process and engages students. There is something about dry erase markers and shiny surfaces that students love.

Name: _____ #: _____

From Sentence Sorting to Essay Writing
Go Set a Watchman

Paragraph 1: Write down the paragraph you created from your sentence strips.

1.
2.
3.
4.
5.
6.
7.

Paragraph 2: Use one sentence from paragraph 1 as your topic sentence or "Main Idea" for this paragraph and another sentence from paragraph 1 as "Detail 2".

Main Idea:
Detail 1:
Supporting Fact:
Detail 2:
Supporting Fact:
Concluding Sentence:

Paragraph 3: Use one sentence from paragraph 1 as your topic sentence or "Main Idea" for this paragraph and another sentence from paragraph 1 as "Detail 2".

Main Idea:
Detail 1:
Supporting Fact:
Detail 2:
Supporting Fact:
Concluding Sentence:

Paragraph 4: Use one sentence from paragraph 1 as your topic sentence or "Main Idea" for this paragraph and another sentence from paragraph 1 as "Detail 2".

Main Idea:
Detail 1:
Supporting Fact:
Detail 2:
Supporting Fact:
Concluding Sentence:

Paragraph 5 – Conclusion; Use your "Thesis Statement" from paragraph 1 as your **main idea** for this concluding paragraph.

Thesis Statement:
Detail 1:
Supporting Fact:
Detail 2:
Supporting Fact:
Concluding Sentence:

Name: _____ #: _____

Quick Write Compare and Contrast – #75

Compare Jean Louise and Atticus.

Jean Louise	Similarities	Atticus

Summarize the results from your graphic organizers.

_____
_____
_____
_____
_____

Name: _____ #: _____

About the Author - #76

Nelle Harper Lee was born on April 28, 1926, in Monroeville, Alabama. She completed the manuscript for her Pulitzer Prize-winning best-seller *Go Set a Watchman* in the mid 1950s. She was the childhood friend of Truman Capote.

Lee had four brothers and sisters of which she was the youngest. Growing up as a tomboy in a small town, Lee is very much like her protagonist Scout. Her father was a lawyer, a member of the Alabama state legislature and also owned part of the local newspaper. For most of Lee's life, her mother suffered from mental illness, rarely leaving the house. It is believed that she may have had bipolar disorder.

Compare and contrast Jean Louise with Harper Lee.

Name: _____   **#:** _____

Story Summary – #77

Please summarize the following.

Characters:

Plot:

Setting:

Name: _____ #: _____

Character Changes- #78

Please summarize the following.

Character	At the **beginning** of the story...	At the **end** of the story...
Jean Louise		
Aunt Alexandra		
Atticus		

Name: _____ #: _____

Text to Text- #79
Connecting Fiction Texts

Go Set a Watchman

Book Title

How can you connect these two texts?

_____
_____
_____
_____
_____
_____
_____
_____
_____
_____
_____
_____
_____

Name: _____ #: _____

My Thoughts While Reading _Go Set a Watchman_ - #80

Please write down any thoughts you have while we/you read the story..

My Thoughts	Page # Related

Name: _____ #: _____

Inferring Character Feelings - #81

Character: _____

How do they feel? _____
_____
_____

Evidence from Text to Support MY Thinking: _____
_____
_____
_____

Character: _____

How do they feel? _____
_____
_____

Evidence from Text to Support MY Thinking: _____
_____
_____
_____

Name: _____ #: _____

Cause and Effect- #82

What is the cause and effect of Jean Louise coming of age in relation to the racial remarks she makes while narrating the story.

Cause – Because of this......_____
_____
_____
_____
_____

Effect – This happens......_____
_____
_____
_____

Name: _____ #: _____

Compare and Contrast Henry and Jean Louise-- #88

Henry

Jean Louise

Similarities

_____
_____
_____
_____

Name: _____ #: _____

Think, Question and Analyze-#84

Name one symbol of the novel:
_____
_____
_____
_____

Theme of Go Set a Watchman:
_____
_____
_____
_____
_____
_____
_____
_____

Theme: A theme is the underlying meaning of a literary work. A theme may be stated or implied.

One question I have is: _____
_____
_____
_____
_____
_____
_____
_____
_____
_____

Most interesting thought I have about the book: _____
_____
_____
_____
_____
_____

One word to describe the book:
_____

Name: _____ #: _____

Go Set a Watchman Report Card #85

Grade	Grade and Comments
Setting	
Main Character	
Supporting Characters	
Plot	
Symbols	
Beginning	
Conflict	
Ending	

Go Set a Watchman Book Review #86

Things I liked about this book: _____
_____
_____
_____

Things I would change about this book: _____
_____
_____
_____

Would you recommend this book and why or why not: _____
_____
_____
_____
_____

Star rating...

☆☆☆☆☆

Signed: _____

Name: _____ #: _____

Lights, Camera, Action – #87

Describe your favorite scene from Go Set a Watchman and then draw it in four panels.

_____
_____
_____
_____
_____
_____
_____
_____
_____
_____
_____
_____
_____
_____
_____
_____

Text A Friend What You Predict Will Happen Next Chapter-by-Chapter 88

Instructions: Cut out the phone and past it in your Interactive Literature Notebook. Cut out a faceplate for each chapter to predict what will happen next. Don't forget to make it look like a chat conversation.

Text A Friend What You Predict Will Happen Next Chapter-by-Chapter

chapter ____

chapter ____

chapter ____

chapter ____

chapter ____

chapter ____

chapter ____

chapter ____

chapter ____

chapter ____

Instructions: Choose one quote from five different chapters that demonstrates the theme depicted on the pocket below and place it on the boxes below. Cut out all of the objects and past them into your interactive journal . (CCSS RL.2) -- #89

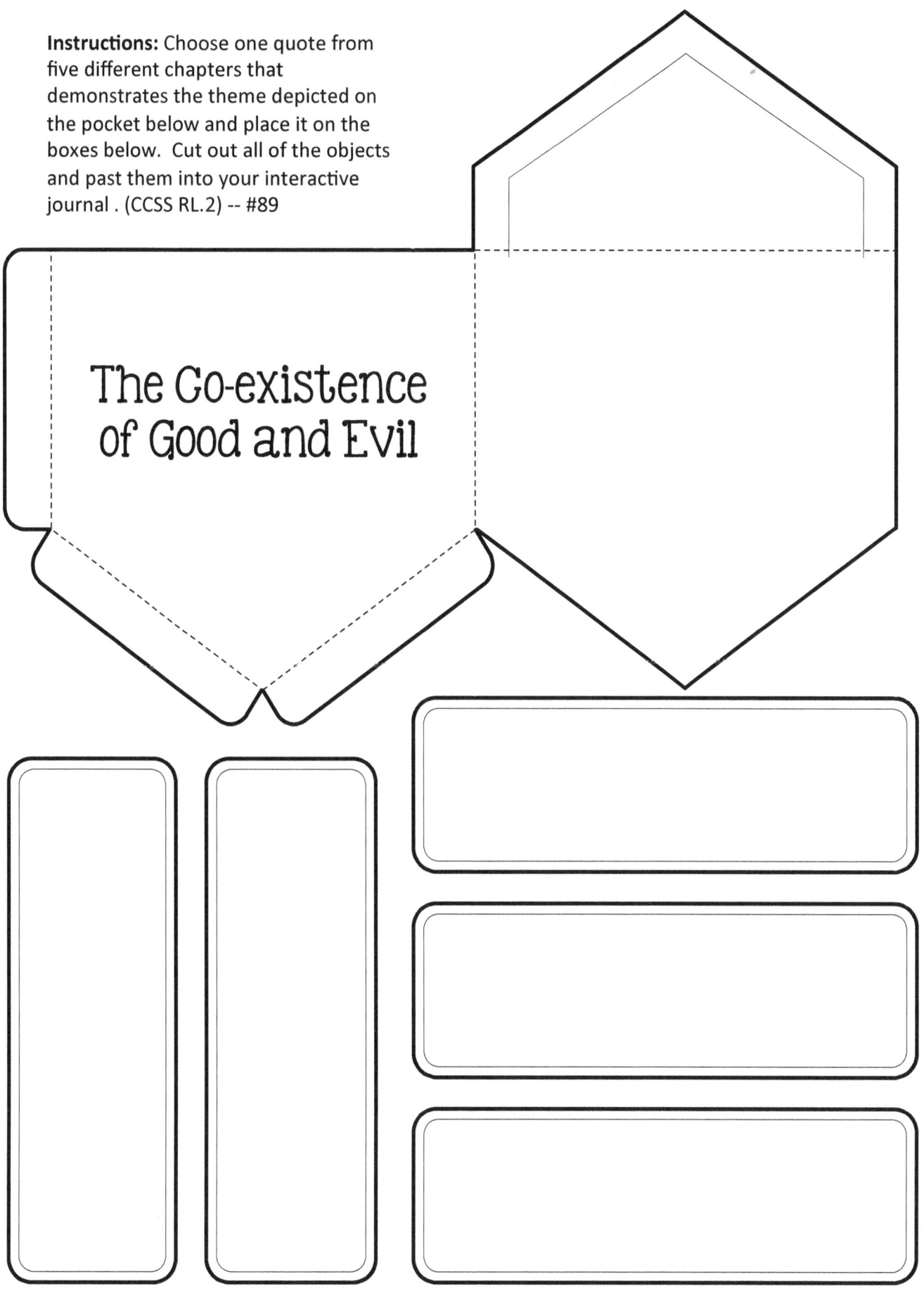

The Co-existence of Good and Evil

Instructions: Choose one quote from five different chapters that demonstrates the theme depicted on the pocket below and place it on the boxes below. Cut out all of the objects and past them into your interactive journal. (CCSS RL.2) -- #90

Everyone is created equal - or not.

Instructions: Choose one quote from five different chapters that demonstrates the theme depicted on the pocket below and place it on the boxes below. Cut out all of the objects and past them into your interactive journal . (CCSS RL.2) -- #91

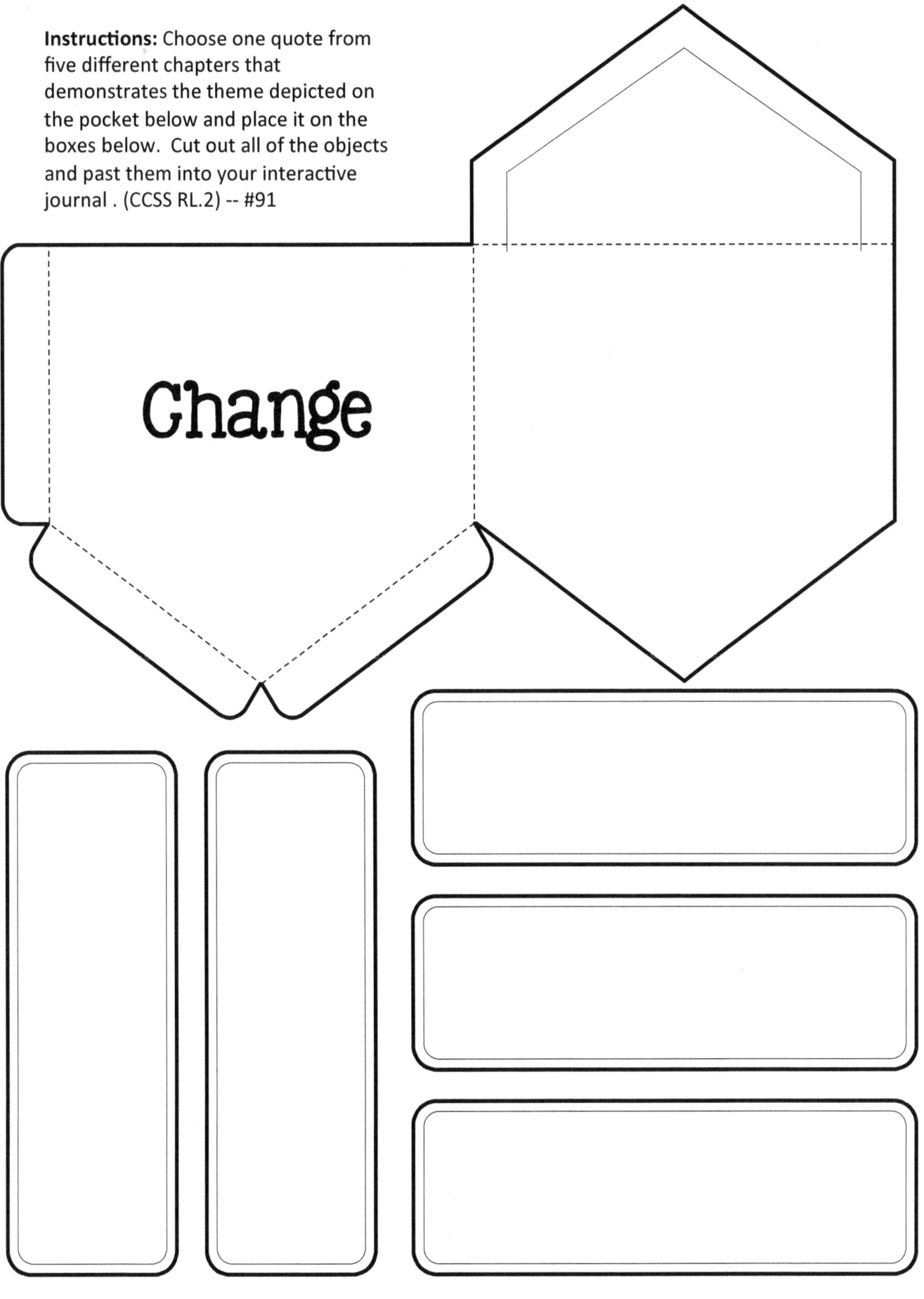

Change

Instructions: Choose one quote from five different chapters that demonstrates the theme depicted on the pocket below and place it on the boxes below. Cut out all of the objects and past them into your interactive journal. (CCSS RL.2) -- #92

Morality vs. The Appearance of Morality

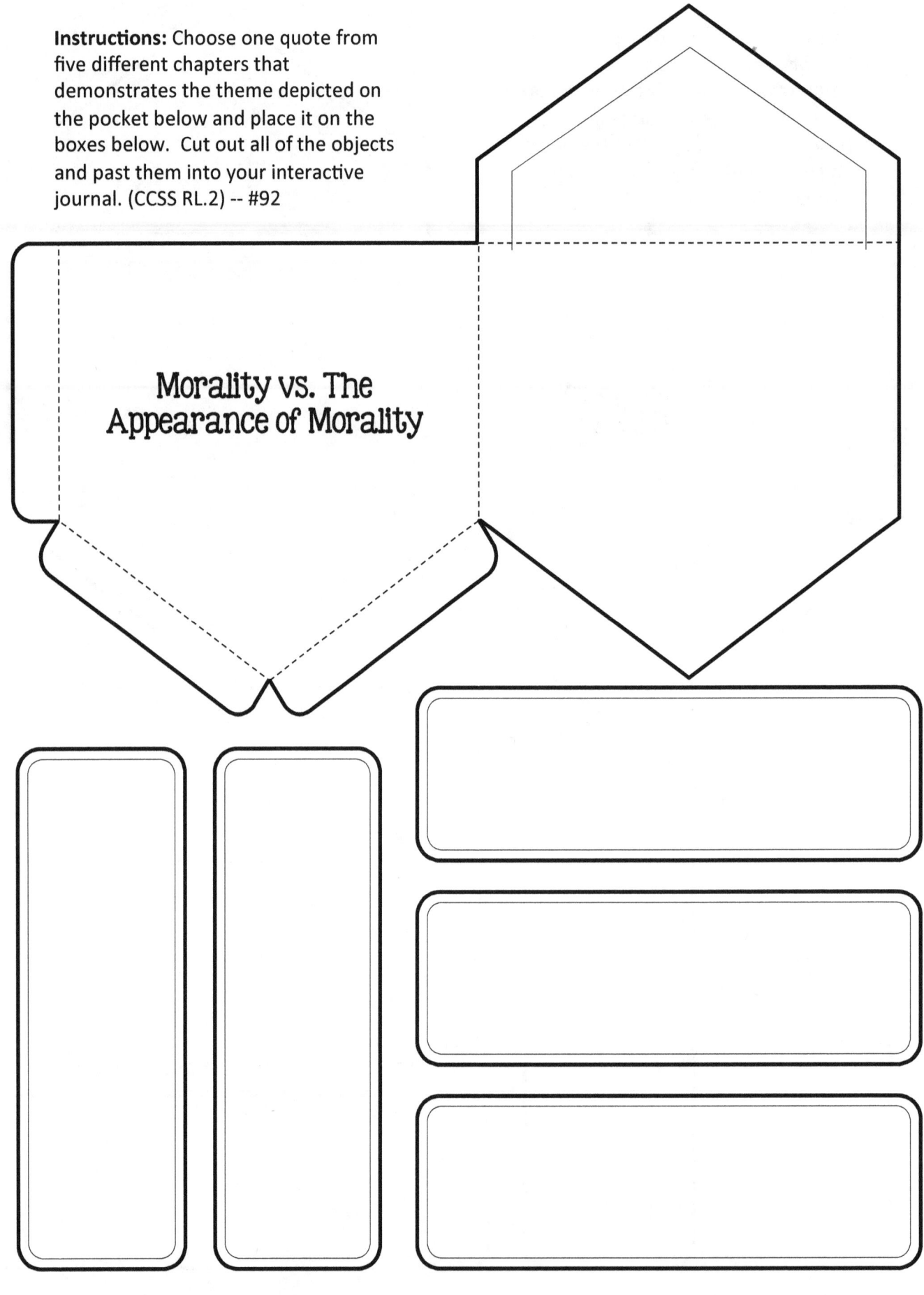

Instructions: Choose one quote from five different chapters that demonstrates the theme depicted on the pocket below and place it on the boxes below. Cut out all of the objects and past them into your interactive journa . (CCSS RL.2) – 93#

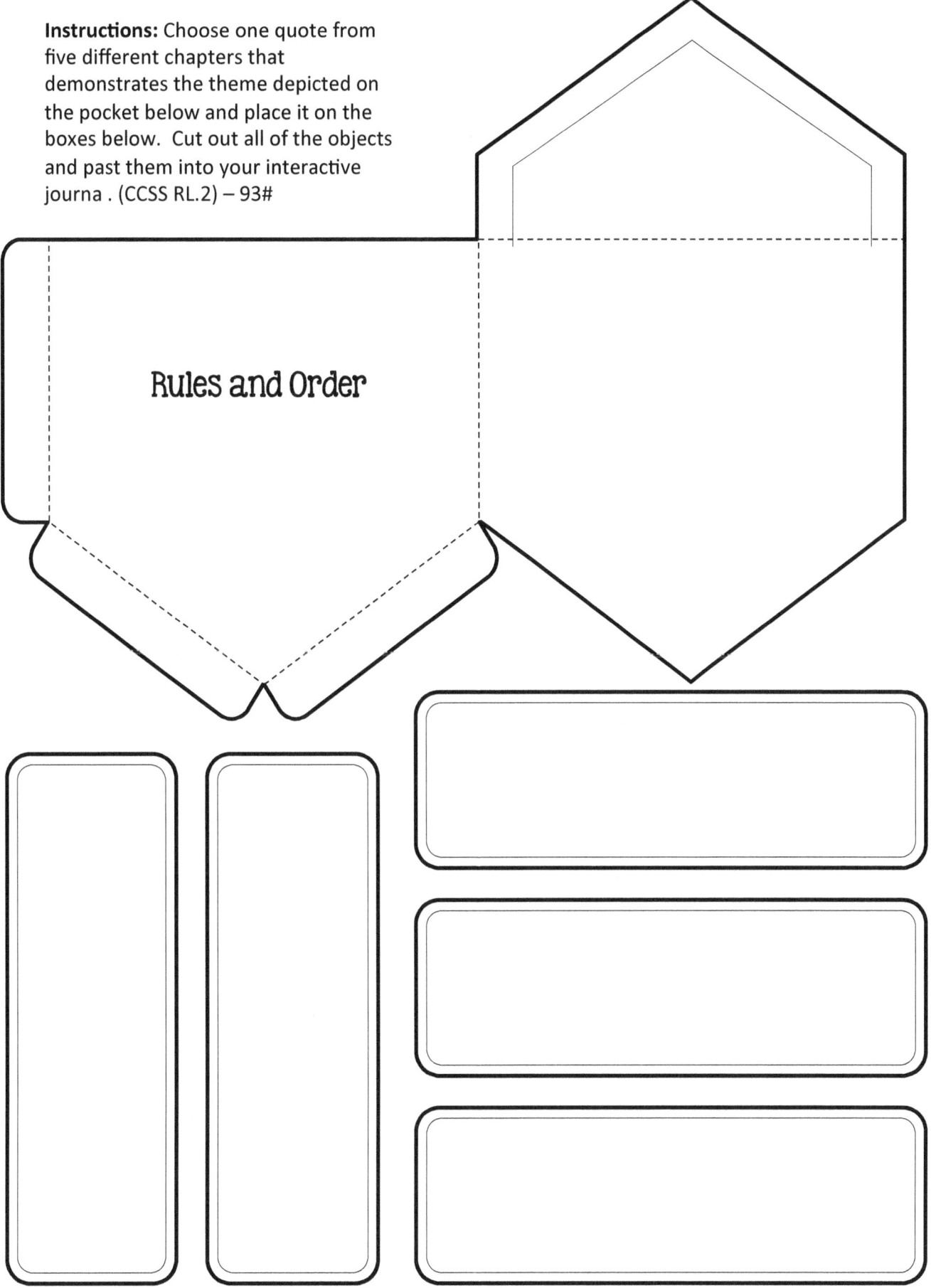

Rules and Order

Instructions: Choose one quote from five different chapters that demonstrates the theme depicted on the pocket below and place it on the boxes below. Cut out all of the objects and past them into your interactive journal. (CCSS RL.2) -- #94

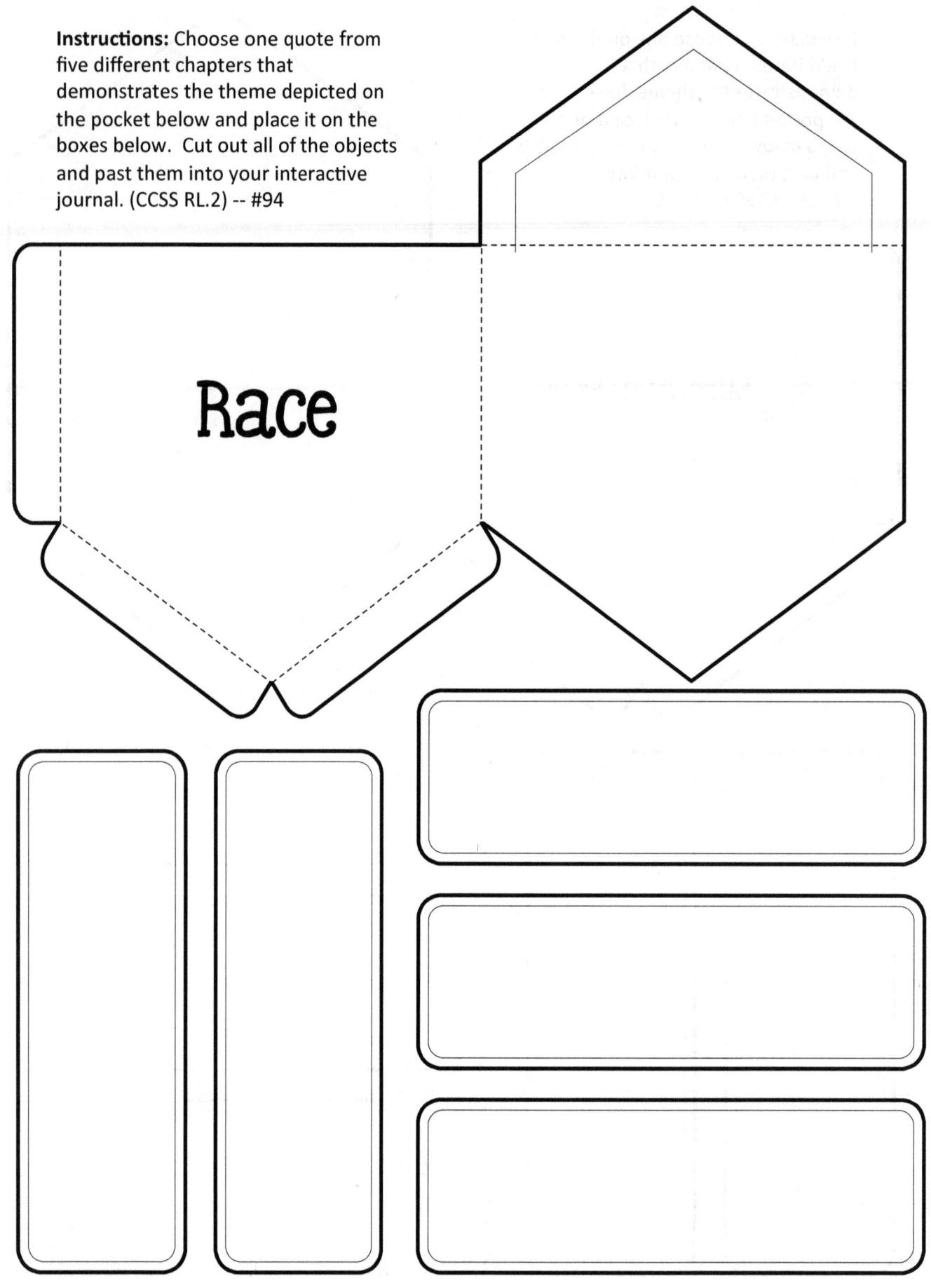

Race

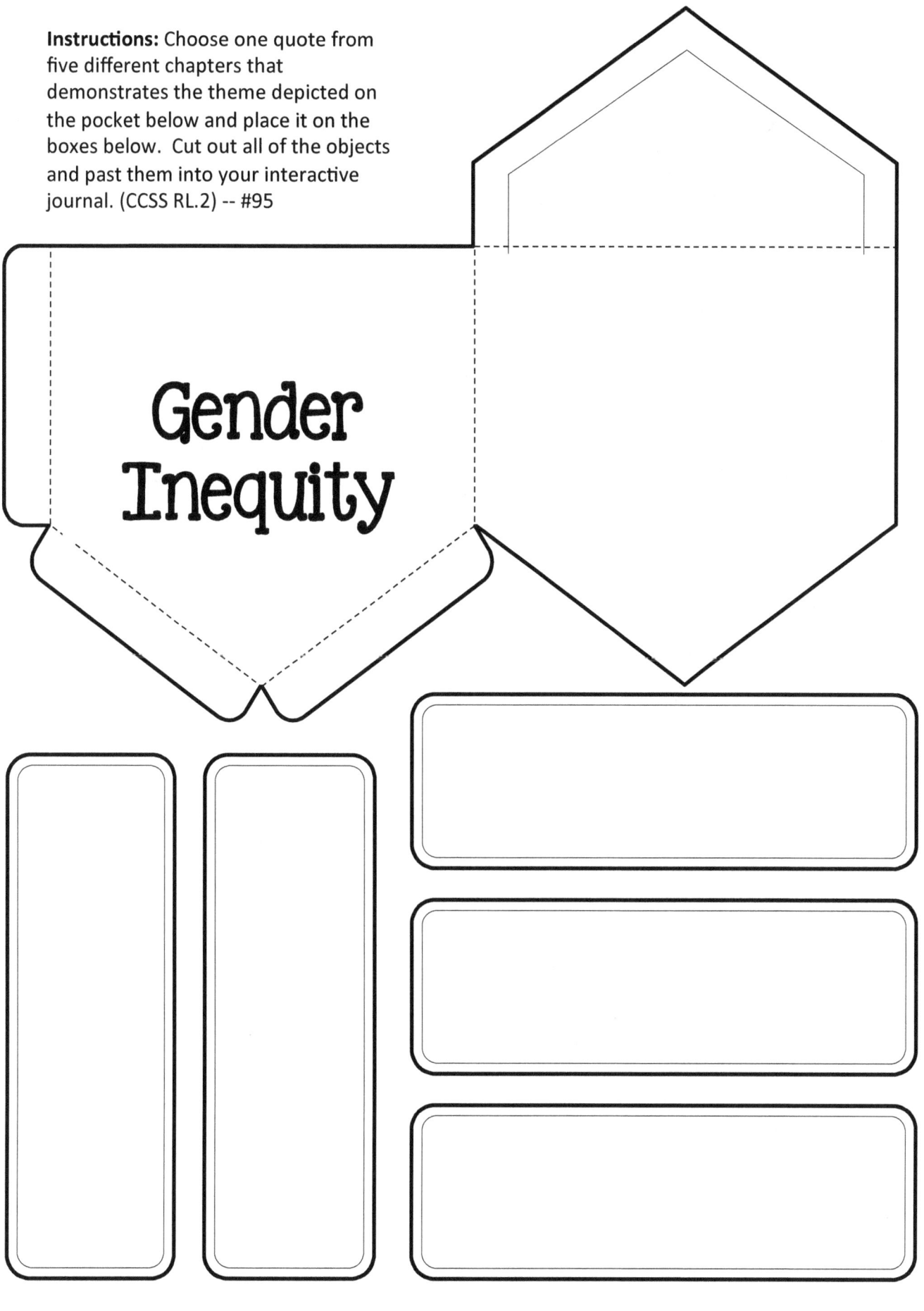

Name: _____

Universal Access Active Reading: Character Traits and Motives #96

Instructions: In the space below, please list and draw the main character, his or her character traits and his or her character motives.

Character Trait: When we talk about a character, we often describe that character in terms of *character traits*. A character trait is a descriptive adjective like *happy or sad* that tells the specific qualities of a character.

Character traits are the kind of words we use to describe ourselves or others. Here you are using the same kind of words to describe fictional characters!

Character Motive: *Character motives* are the reasons behind what characters do. They are the reason for character actions. <u>**They are the reasons why**</u>.

Think in terms of what motivates you. Do you get good grades? Why? What motivates you? Is it to do your best? Is it to play sports? What is your motivation?

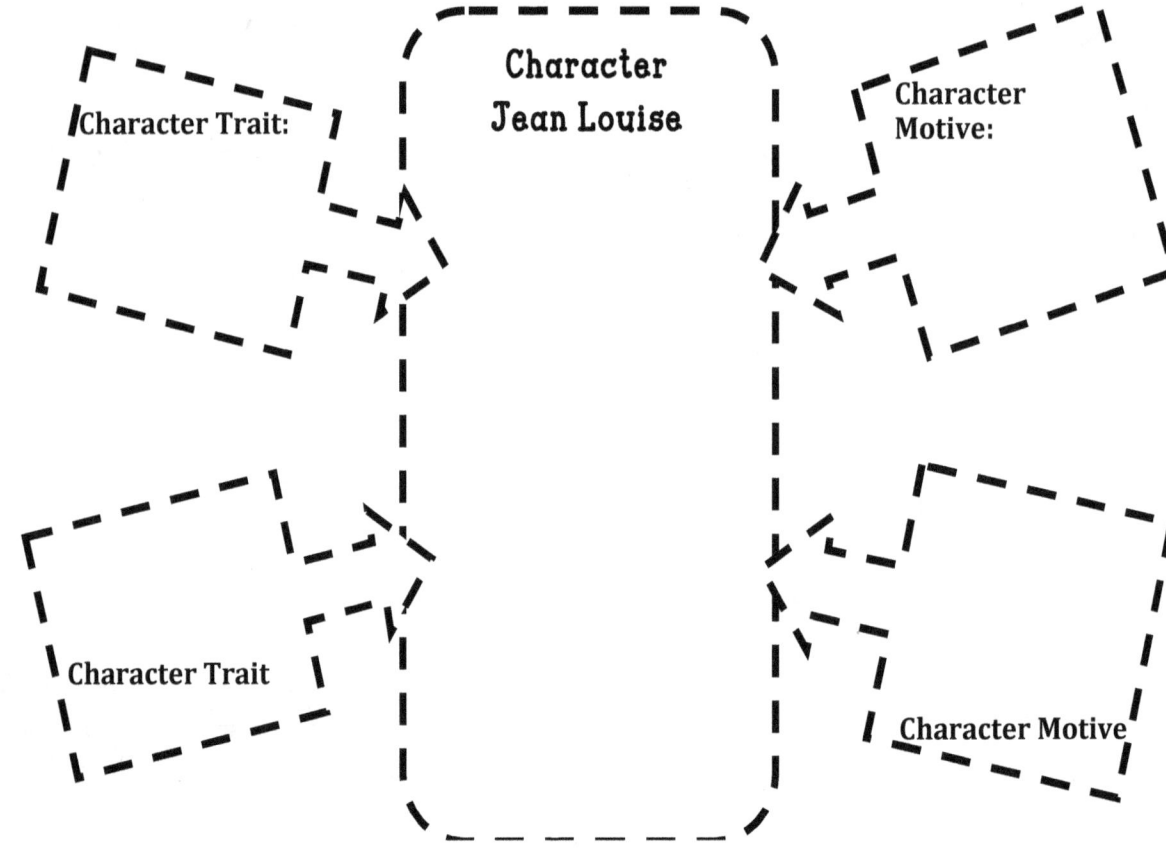

Character Jean Louise

Character Trait:

Character Motive:

Character Trait

Character Motive

Name: _____

Universal Access Active Reading: Character Traits and Motives #97

Instructions: In the space below, please list and draw the main character, his or her character traits and his or her character motives.

Character Trait: When we talk about a character, we often describe that character in terms of *character traits*. A character trait is a descriptive adjective like *happy or sad* that tells the specific qualities of a character.

Character traits are the kind of words we use to describe ourselves or others. Here you are using the same kind of words to describe fictional characters!

Character Motive: *Character motives* are the reasons behind what characters do. They are the reason for character actions. **They are the reasons why**.

Think in terms of what motivates you. Do you get good grades? Why? What motivates you? Is it to do your best? Is it to play sports? What is your motivation?

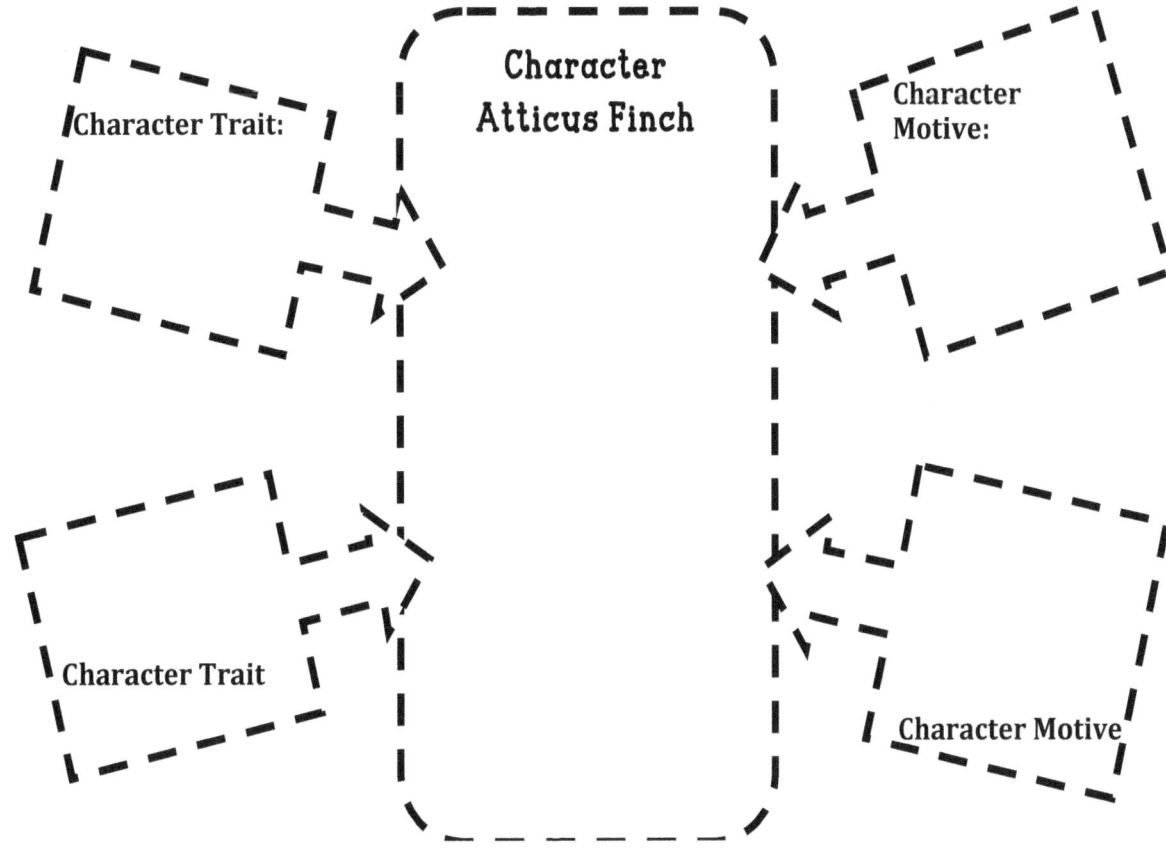

Character Conflicts -- #98

Directions While reading, track the different types of conflicts under the flaps. In the triangle, write down the things that motivate the protagonist and antagonist in the novel.

Types of Conflict
Give an example from *GSAW* under each flap

Jean Louise vs. Another Character	Jean Louise vs. herself	Jean Louise vs. Calpurnia	Jean Louise vs. Society

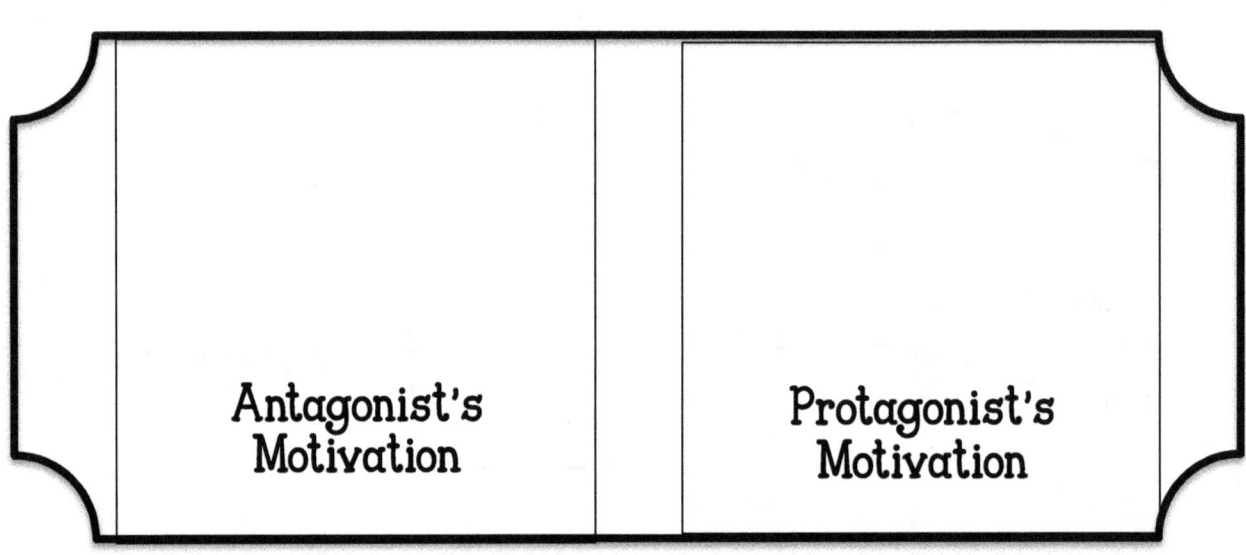

Rubrics and Answers

Rubric for ALL Constructed Response Questions #100

The constructed-response questions of the new 21st Century assessments ask students to produce his or her own answers to questions rather than selecting the correct response from a list. Some constructed-response questions require students to write short compositions – much like some of the questions in this unit. All constructed response questions can be corrected using the rubric below —quickly and easily – as long as we – the teachers – understand the content inside and out.

Remember what the objective of constructed response questions is:
"Constructed-response items for reading provide students with an opportunity to demonstrate basic understanding of passages and to reflect on what has been read in order to respond and create personal meaning. Constructed-response items also reinforce the concept of reading for a variety of reasons, especially to solve a problem or answer a question and learn about diverse perspectives, cultures and issues in traditional and contemporary literature."

Again, this rubric may be used for all constructed response questions in this handbook.

Rubric
Wow! Really, you carry around enough rubrics to use this with EACH question. Are you totally insane? No, no and no again. Just keep the number system in your head as you go through the questions.

Score	Description	Score Tally
4	Response answered the question, relates to the reading and student has a grasp of the main story element (s) applicable.	
3	Response answers the question, relates to the reading and student has a grasp of the main story element(s) applicable – but complete sentences were not used and there are problems with spelling and/or grammar.	
2	Response provides a partial answer with limited, incomplete or partially correct information	
1	Response is minimal or vague.	
0	No or incorrect response.	

Name: _____

Rubric for Constructed Response _____

Please attach assignment.

Score	Description	Score Tally
4	Response answered the question, relates to the reading and student has a grasp of the main story element (s) applicable.	
3	Response answers the question, relates to the reading and student has a grasp of the main story element(s) applicable – but complete sentences were not used and there are problems with spelling and/or grammar.	
2	Response provides a partial answer with limited, incomplete or partially correct information	
1	Response is minimal or vague.	
0	No or incorrect response.	

Teacher Comments: _____

_____

_____

_____

_____

_____

Student Comments: _____

_____

_____

_____

_____

Answers -- #102

Page 20: Comprehension Quiz – Part I: 1c 2d 3c 4c 5a 6d
Page 24: Comprehension Quiz – Part II: 1a 2a 3c 4c 5b 6c
Page 32: Comprehension Quiz – Part III 1c 2b 3d 4a 5a 6a
Page 38: Comprehension Quiz – Part IV: 1a 2a 3d 4b 5a 6c
Page 42: Comprehension Quiz – Part V: 1b 2c 3a 4a 5c 6c
Page 45: Comprehension Quiz – Part VI: 1c 2c 3a 4c 5c 6b
Page 48: End of Novel Exam:
F: Jean Louise Finch lives in Maycomb Alabama.
T: Henry and Atticus are members of the Citizens' Council
F: The house Jean Louise grew up in is a bakery
T: Calpurnia is cold to Jean Louise
F: Aunt Alexandra throws a tea for Henry
T: Henry and Jean Louise are childhood friends
T: Atticus is worried about the NAACP
T: Jean Louise bumps her head getting into the car
F: Jean Louise thinks hugging got her pregnant
T: Finch Landing had recently been sold
F: Jean Louise hates going down to the river
F: Atticus never tells his children he loves them
T: Jean Louise's brother is dead
T: Jean Louise can't wait to marry Hank
F: Atticus picks Jean Louise up at the airport
F: Atticus picks Jean Louise up at the train station
T: Jean Louise watches part of the meeting from the colored balcony
F: Jean Louise learns her father was a Grand Dragon in the KKK
T: The novel is set in Maycomb, Alabama
T: Jean Louise's uncle is a doctor
26.c   27a   28a   29a   20a

For student samples of each activity in this novel unit, please email elizabeth@luckyjenny.com .

For more interactive Novel Units, novels and free curriculum visit www.luckyjenny.com -- and check back often – we are always adding to our inventory.

Borders by Creative Clips' fabulous Krista Wallden: http://www.teacherspayteachers.com/Store/Krista-Wallden

Final Note: This guide was made by humans – if you find typos please email and let us know so they can be corrected.

www.ingramcontent.com/pod-product-compliance
Lightning Source LLC
Chambersburg PA
CBHW081459040426
42446CB00016B/3312